For my mother Lee and my father Edward.

Teaching and Writing Popular Fiction: Horror, Adventure, Mystery and Romance in the American Classroom

Karen M. Hubert

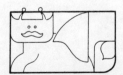

Teachers&Writers

84 Fifth Avenue, New York, New York 10011

The publication of this book is made possible by a grant from the Na-
tional Endowment for the Arts.

Third Printing 1978

Contents

PART FIVE: ROMANCE

ANTHOLOGY

Introduction

In graduate school I was continually exposed to literature of the highest order: great and serious books on love and death, conflict and adventure. As a result, I came to believe that the only kind of literature worth reading had been written by geniuses like Shakespeare, Dostoevsky, and Goethe. It followed that only one kind of literature should be produced: classics. As a young writer I felt that for a work of mine to have value it would need to be as great as that of my Olympian predecessors. But Dickens and George Eliot were stiff competition, and I found myself questioning even my right to write. If my first paragraph wasn't up to the standards of the Great American Novel, I'd toss it away and scrap the project. There existed only superb or awful writing, nothing in between. So I stopped writing.

I also stopped reading. Faulkner and Tolstoy served only to highlight my inadequacies. Their every word was a cruel reminder that my own talent was no match for theirs. I never regarded this reaction as healthy, but I was stuck with my condition and had to nurse it as best I could.

I was like someone with an allergy. Good books made me sick. At first I stayed away from my old haunts. Bookstores, libraries, even my living-room bookshelves were off limits. But half a year later, I weakened. I found myself drawn to those racks in supermarkets and bus and train terminals that offer popular fiction. The only books that I was able to read painlessly at first were those I found in drugstore bins and generally regarded by serious readers as junk: mysteries, gothics, romances, adventures, science fiction and westerns. I made more and more trips to bigger and better drugstores, and the more I read the better I liked what I was reading and the more I wanted to read.

I discovered Jacqueline Susann, Irving Wallace, Susan Howatch, and some old writers whose works were once considered pulp but have since become minor classics: Raymond Chandler, Dashiell Hammett, Margaret Mitchell. Through this "middle ground" literature, I came to understand the merits of writing as entertainment, the power and importance of story, plot, and reader involvement. I rediscovered the pleasure of wanting to know what happened next. I had to admit that these books, although not great by any definition of the word, were moving, entertaining, and satisfying. Once I realized that popular literature had value, my own gifts became available to me again: I was unblocked. My stories *didn't* have to be works of genius; they had only to be the best I could do.

The change in my reading tastes affected my teaching. Curious to know what my students read, I discovered that they too liked popular genres. I made several trips to the school library for nostalgia's sake and found some old friends. Nancy Drew was still snooping, the Hardy Boys were still having adventures, the Black Stallion hadn't stopped kicking, and Beverly Cleary's *Fifteen* was as soppy as ever. These books were well worn and appeared to have been thoroughly enjoyed by many readers.

How could I get my students to enjoy writing this much?

They didn't read these books because they had to, but because they wanted to. What connection could I make between reading, an activity in which they knew what they liked, and writing, an activity that they didn't like very much? Why not provide writing ideas that echoed their reading preferences?

This book attempts to answer such questions. It is meant for any teacher interested in expanding her writing curriculum. I've included some theoretical background on the nature and emotional content of each of the four popular genres I treat. The teacher should use this information to supplement my practical suggestions of writing ideas. These "recipes" have been tried and tested—by other teachers as well as myself at the elementary, high school, and college level. Illustrations of student writing are drawn from a wide range of ages. I have introduced genre projects at P.S. 75 in Manhattan, P.M. High School in Brooklyn, and at Staten Island Community College. At the college and high school I worked with my own classes. At P.S. 75 I worked within other teachers' classes as well as with smaller groups composed of one to fifteen children.

I would like to thank Teachers & Writers Collaborative and in particular Steve Schrader for giving me the opportunity and the room to pursue an individual and experimental approach to the teaching of writing. My friend Phillip Lopate who suggested that the Genre Project be made into a book. It is typical of his generous and supportive spirit. And Leonard Allison of Total Effect, Resources for Education, who many years ago introduced me to the notion of Genre and showed me that making reading and writing real and accessible to students is a statement of our belief in them.

The Genre Approach

Why Genre?

You believe in the value of student writing. You are committed to providing a large and interesting writing curriculum. You purchase pamphlets and books like this one. You subscribe to magazines in search of ways to help your students write out of personal inclination rather than because they are compelled to. You are trying to find ideas that will work.

A writing assignment works when it fully captures the writer's imagination, when the assignment evokes personal fantasies. Fantasy is the set of stories a person likes to tell herself whenever an occasion arises for escape. But imaginations are as various as the people they inhabit. Usually when we give a writing assignment it works for only some of our students. To reach everyone in a class of thirty-five, we would have to come up with thirty-five different writing exercises. But even if we had the time, how could we determine the predilections of one imagination, let alone thirty-five?

Yet there are clues we can seek. Consider the areas in which your students continually express their personalities and tastes: in the games they play, in the books and comics they read, in the television shows and movies they watch. By a very early age, they have well-defined preferences. Their choices are directly related to their imaginations. If we observe the kinds of choices made by students in entertaining themselves, we will discover clear-cut taste patterns. Awareness of these patterns can be very useful to us in devising writing ideas that will work for the great majority of our students.

At the library, one student picks only family sagas, another goes right to the mystery shelf, one inspects all the romances, others congregate in the adventure section, while some pick fantasies, ghost stories, westerns. An occasional student, less fussy, can find entertainment in nearly any yarn.

Your children watch one television program instead of another. Given a choice between two nearby theaters, one showing a romance that promises lots of kisses and the other a scream-filled horror movie, a student naturally will prefer one to the other. In school or after-school activities, she will choose to play certain roles or games according to her own particular preference for speed, grace, domesticity or violence.

In every instance of self-expression and choice, your student is ruled by an undercurrent of personal fantasy, by the story teller who lives in each one of us. Every student comes to class carrying a volume of stories all her own. She likes to act, read or see many versions of the same story in order to re-experience the particular emotions she most needs or likes to feel. She will view these stories, read them and play them any chance she gets. And she would write them down if she were only given the framework and the opportunity.

Although a child generally recognizes her freedom of choice where entertainment is concerned, she is not conscious that this same choice is available to her in her writing. A child chooses one book over others on the basis of two things: the desire to experience one fantasy as opposed to another and the ease with which she can identify with the voices of the narrator and characters. If she can read the words to herself with feeling, the book comes alive for her. She may actually hear "Golly Mom, do I have to?" better than "Stick 'em up, you fool!" A romance and a mystery, for example, differ widely in voice, language, structure, images, and heroic values:

> "She felt the love in every line of his frame flow into hers, she knew he would never again belong to anyone except her."
> (Susan Howatch *Dark Shore*, p. 217)

> "I parked my crate on the street. A hard-eyed Filipino in a white coat curled his lip at me."
> (Raymond Chandler, *The High Window*, p. 29)

Among the plagiarisms from encyclopedias and the too-simple sentences of book reports, a teacher occasionally runs across a phrase or statement that is charming and fresh. This is voice: behind the writing one feels the presence of a distinct personality. A child's voice emerges the most clearly when she is writing about something she knows or likes. A student does not see that writing can be a form of self-entertainment because it fails to come up to her favorite experiences. "My life as a Hamster" is somehow too far removed from Spider-Man comics and *The Towering Inferno*.

Children are familiar, by the remarkably early age of seven or eight, with nearly all the literary forms: poems, diaries, fiction, essays, biographies, interviews and book reviews. The subject matter of their assigned writing is eclectic, chosen from such topics as "George Washington Carver," "Christmas Vacation," "How Sugar Cane Is Harvested," "I Woke Up One Morning As a Pencil." Despite the great variety we offer them, for the most part our students write to entertain us, not themselves. We tend to lose sight of the variety of literary forms with which they themselves are familiar.

By the time a student has started school she has encountered every major story "family" or genre—adventure, romance, mystery, horror—as well as story types that fall into these categories such as fantasy, science fiction, westerns and gothics. She knows best of all the hybrid story: romance-adventure, mystery-horror, science fiction-adventure-mystery, etc. These are legitimate forms, and they should be studied in our classrooms. By offering students the same kind of choices available to them in their other entertainment, teachers can begin to turn writing into self-entertainment.

"But shouldn't we try to introduce 'good' literature, the classics? Don't we want to elevate our students' tastes?" We all have different theories as to how cultural enrichment can be made part of the curriculum. But we need a starting point, and there is no better place to begin than where the children are now, using the taste they have already acquired to encourage their active participation in what they read. Try taking those Hardy boys seriously. Read one of their books as a class project, and discuss it with your students.

There are, of course, differences between classics and works of popular genre. Works of popular genre lack depth: they are born out of current fads and tastes rather than less mortal stuff. Classics reflect larger portions of life. One feels that living has been going on before one opens the book and will continue after one closes it. It gives rise to reflection and a realistic range of emotions and insights. One reads the popular genres to be entertained rather than to be moved and to enjoy a particular satisfaction at the conclusion of a book. In these novels all action moves toward the resolution of a single, limited situation. Will the man and woman get together? Will Philip Marlowe solve the crime? Will Lassie reach the top of the mountain in time to save the young boy?

Popular literature may not touch us as deeply or as profoundly, yet Daphne du Maurier's *Rebecca* is made of the same basic stuff as Charlotte Bronte's *Jane Eyre*. Jakov Lind once said to me that only twelve basic plots exist. If this is true, then a remarkable amount of literature is repetition. Underneath it all it is the momentum of the *story* that must move us before style, philosophy or wit can take over. There is satisfaction in watching a conventional plot unfold, there is beauty and order in everything falling into place—just as the reader expects and hopes it will, with a few surprises here and there.

You will undoubtedly feel the impact of television, movies and media in the stories your students write. Certainly that influence is there, as the hundreds of Kung Fu imitations you read every term have proven. But where did the basic plots behind these television stories originate? Certainly story types have been in existence even before stories were written, ever since stories have been *told*. The basic fantasies at the core of love, adventure, horror and mystery are part of man's basic nature. (If there were no TV, no movies or printed media, people of all ages would still tell stories. And the stories they would tell would fall into these same four categories.)

Your students are naturally romantic, angry, adventurous, anxious and frightened. They pick their entertainment accordingly. The realization that they have this same choice in writing can only help them to express themselves more fully. Through writing and reading popular genres, they come to understand that there are many kinds of stories, and that each type is unique and appropriate to particular feelings. When they feel blue or moody, in a yearning mood, they might try a romance. When they feel angry, they might choose a more violent form—a mystery or adventure story.

I began the Genre Project in an attempt to broaden my students' concept of story and to give them a richer choice of writing possibilities. I thought of the various genres as different shaped jello molds into which different flavors and colors might be poured to set. I introduced my students to the various genres and let them write in all of them. This opportunity enabled the students to see what forms they liked best, felt most comfortable with and could most naturally fit their voices and their feelings into. I emphasized that each genre lent itself to particular emotions. Certain of my students gravitated to certain forms. It was always interesting to see who traveled easily among forms and who concentrated on one in exclusion of others.

Working with genre is a sure way of tailoring writing ideas to fit individual students' personalities. Imagine Johnny, a chronic fighter, a bully who picks on everyone. Excited by Kung Fu, he performs it whenever he can. He is highly competitive. He is angry. Having formed this rather superficial view of Johnny, what shall we as teachers ask him to write? If we were to design an assignment close to his heart, it might be to give a blow-by-blow description of a fight he once saw or engaged in. Chances are, Johnny would do some good writing. But this is just the top of the iceberg. If his fight scene is good, imagine how interesting might be his descriptions of the fighters or his attempts to explain how and why they came to fight. Since Johnny understands the combative spirit so well, why not provide him with the framework in which to write about violence and intrigue? Why not introduce him to the adventure story or perhaps the murder mystery? He might enjoy describing hard-boiled, indestructible detectives, suspects and criminals, police line-ups, and chases, and he may understand the reason and unreason behind motives and the feelings connected with being pursued and getting caught.

Student writing often lacks a defined shape. Even "felt" writing, so valuable because of its emotional or personal content, might be brought a step further, molded from raw expression into refined prose.

Students are conscious of form in every story they encounter in movies, books and TV. To be aware of form is to have a sense of what will happen next. The ability to anticipate means we have internalized form; we have absorbed the elements of a genre into our own imaginative selves. Form, or genre, corresponds to our own inner sense of story logic. A thing happens next because it is right, it fits, it satisfies.

All stories share the element of suspense. As we read along, the story all but compels us to hope or want a certain thing to happen. We want the mountain climber to reach his goal, the ship to get through the icy waters, the detective to escape the criminal who holds him captive. In our heart we know that the mountain climber, ship and detective will make it. Our story intuition tells us that the detective will either cleverly trick his captor or physically overwhelm him, or that he will be rescued by help from the outside. The story sets us up; we want a certain thing to happen, and when it does it hits the spot.

But the forms that our students know so well and that are so much a part of their imaginative process do not function for them when they write in the classroom. Instead, "What should I write next?" and "Is this enough?" are the common questions they ask themselves and us. Unawareness of form only confines a young writer. Acquainted with a genre, a student knows the kinds of things that might go next. A wealth of choices and directions is available to her. Genre opens up doors to the young writer; it does not offer formulas. When a student writes an adventure story, she faces the challenge of putting into words courage, fear and other emotions and feelings associated with risk-taking. A student who writes a mystery must describe suspects, devise motives, detail how the crime was committed. She must learn technique as well, for she has to keep her readers guessing. Rather then restricting students, form opens up possibilities for them.

The following piece of student writing has all the seeds of a mystery or a horror story. Its author might have easily developed it into a long story of either genre:

This was in the first grade. With Edith, Jane, Athie and Ellen. Well, Edith was one of the showoff girls. She always wanted to show the girls that she was the best in the class. She always picked on one of the nicest girls named Jackie. Athie was another one also. One day at lunch time Athie was picking on Jackie, the poor nice girl. Then it was Edith. You see, Ellen and Jane always told the girls to pick on me.

So the following day I played a trick on all the girls. I put a rat in their desk and when they took out their books the fake rat fell on the floor. They screamed like hell. They were looking for the snotty girl who did the trick. So they found out it was you know who. So they said, I am sorry Jackie, we learned a lesson.

This tale of revenge has motive, crime, suspects, victims and a solution: in short, all the elements needed for a mystery. Looked at in psychological terms, it is an example of wish-fulfillment in which a past hurt is relived and then dealt with imaginatively. Writing fiction is invaluable for young students because it allows them to confront and give shape to their experience. For the teacher, working with genre provides viable alternatives and variety in the teaching of creative writing, and gives legitimacy to forms and subjects with which students are already familiar.

Building Up to Writing Stories

I refer in this book to the "qualities," "elements," "telling," and "writing" of genre stories. These four categories are part of an easy and successful approach to teaching genre. The categories may be treated separately or as a unit. As a unit, they form what I call the "building-up" method. This method is based on the belief that your students are already experts on genre, through their reading, viewing and fantasizing, and through their personal experiences. The teacher's aim is to use all the information already possessed by the students as a basis for teaching.

Qualities. How does a particular type of story make you feel? What makes a horror story a horror story and not a romance? Each genre elicits a unique response from readers. Your students have responded to genres many times, but they may not be aware of the differences between them. To get at the uniqueness of a genre, ask your students how such a story (horror, romance, mystery or adventure) makes them *feel.* Generally, they will reply with adjectives and short descriptive phrases from which the *qualities* of the genre emerge. You'll get such answers as scared, nervous, like I want to run away from it, disgusting, shocking, gory; or mushy, in love, passionate, yearning; or intriguing, mind-boggling, it's like a puzzle, suspicious; or suspenseful, will they make it?, on the edge of my seat, my body tenses up. (If your students begin to tell stories to illustrate their feelings, interrupt them: they'll have a chance to tell these stories later on.) As your students are calling out descriptive words and phrases, you might write them on the blackboard, not in a list but widely scattered to imply in visual terms the number of qualities and the extent and variety of class knowledge.

You may wish to point out particular words or phrases like "disgusting," "nervous," "mushy," "on the edge of my seat," and ask the students if they can tell you more about them; how the words feel in relation to the body, for example. Ask them to make faces or gestures that go with particular words. If one student makes a face naturally, draw attention to it: "What a scary face you just made as you said that word! Can anyone else make a face to go with that word?" Try to bring out the sense of a word like "yuckky" that they already show in their bodies, faces and gestures.

The naming or listing of qualities should serve as an introduction to the world you will be asking your students to think, imagine, live and write in. It is a kind of orientation; a way of showing students that they are entering a unique imaginative terrain that has a special effect on the readers and writers who pass through it.

Elements. What are the components of different kinds of stories? What kinds of things happen in them? You are investigating, here, parts of stories, pieces of plot, bits of situations. Elements include action, events, props, sounds, settings, types of characters, types of surprises, gestures, and so on.

A list of elements in any one genre is endless. In a horror story, they would include monsters, ghosts, haunted houses, a cackling laugh, echoes, insanity, a room full of mirrors, a mean old man, things jumping out unexpectedly, a mad scientist, ringed eyes, wrinkled skin, claws, blood, a clock striking midnight, a swamp, cemeteries, coffins. In a romance: a kiss, a hug, looking into someone's eyes, a long walk on the beach, moonlight, a marriage proposal, a jealous boyfriend, a rival, a disapproving parent, a double date, holding hands at the movies, a dark place, candlelight, red lips, an uptilted face, a honeymoon.

Elements of a mystery include a victim, a murder, a stolen vase, a butler, a detective, a policeman, a gun, a knife, a rope, a hiding place, a chase, a shootout, capture of the criminal, interrogations, witnesses, suspects, jail, gangsters. Of an adventure: a treasure, a mountain, a river, a snowstorm, a waterfall, a canoe, a rescue, breakdown of a car in the middle of a desert, a kidnaping, a journey, a race, a sailboat, a high wind, loss of control, fear, worry, doubt as to whether you'll reach your goal or get back home, a lucky break, a feeling of satisfaction, bravery, courage.

Once this listing of elements begins, it snowballs very quickly. A student is excited to discover and share her expertise. She realizes how familiar she is with a genre without ever having studied it. And she is excited to find that her own cultural experiences have value to her teacher and her classmates. For this reason, a lesson in "collecting" elements can be intense, with lots of yelling out and laughing. I think that in this instance such unrestrained energy is desirable. If the experience has been rollicking and high-pitched you might ask your students whether they noticed the level of energy and enthusiasm in the room. How do they account for it? Where did it come from? By the way, when you work in romance, the humor may be more embarrassed, and the energy more muted. This restraint, too, poses interesting possibilities for class discussion.

I usually don't list elements on the blackboard. For one thing, writing them tends to diminish the energy level and the class's sense of participation. (Instead I often enter them in a notebook, to refer to if my students get stuck writing their stories and need suggestions.) For another, students may rely on the list rather than using their own powers of retention and creative imagination.

Telling. How many types of stories does a genre consist of? How many plots are there? In this lesson, students tell as many stories within the genre as they can. It's a good idea to turn the lesson into a game in which one story may not duplicate the last. Similar elements may be used, or not, if you want to make the game very hard. A chase, for example, might turn up in several stories, but not a chase to the same location, or with the same characters. Plots may be offered by individuals, by groups, or by the whole class, round robin. If one story sounds like another, ask the teller or the class to make something different happen in it by introducing a new and different *element.* The stories the class tells may be real or fictitious.

You may wish to give each kind of story a name or a title and write it on the board, to bring home the point that types or *conventions* exist within a genre. For example, in the adventure genre there are kidnap stories, journey stories, stories of man against the elements. In romance, love at first sight, betrayal, and unrequited love are types of stories. Horror has monster stories, stories of creatures from outer space, psychotic-human stories. Mysteries may include murder mysteries, espionage mysteries, mysteries in which an attempt is made to prevent a crime, mysteries concerning stolen objects.

The naming or titling process is optional. The pitfall is obvious; students may think of the titles as rules to which their stories must conform. It must be carefully explained that these are types, not rules. For some students the titling process is a step toward further consciousness and control over material. Others disregard it or don't profit from it.

Writing. After telling, writing a story is an easy step.

Having pooled all their knowledge and experience, students and the teacher are familiar with the genres. You may choose right away to ask your students to write according to an idea in this book, or you may just want to ask them to write their *own* idea of a mystery, romance, horror or adventure story.

By now they will have much material from class discussions and their own imaginations. Explain that elements and types of stories may be mixed in any way, just as white cake batter and chocolate batter may be mixed to make a new kind of marble cake. After the stories are written, student or teacher may wish to read them aloud. Some may be typed and mimeographed. I've found that students enjoy such booklets tremendously and that distributing them is one of the best ways to encourage writing.

One may stay in any of the four parts of the building-up method—qualities, elements, telling and writing—as long as one wants, and according to class need and interest. Some classes run through the entire sequence in an hour; others take over a month. The exploration of each part is different and adds to the next part.

I suggest that you study one genre at a time. You might do well to begin with the genre you yourself enjoy or understand best. If you notice that the majority of your students are reading primarily in one genre, start there, then move on to the others, one at a time. I like each class or group to experience every genre. I don't necessarily start with the building-up method; rather I present each genre differently so as to avoid repetition. At some point, however, I always introduce qualities and elements. I find these parts essential to the understanding of any genre.

A final reminder: Don't be surprised if some of your students write hybrid stories. Very few stories stay religiously within the confines of their genre. More often one meets such compounds as horror-adventure, mystery-romance, adventure-romance, mystery-horror, and so on. After all, even Charlie Chan had a girlfriend.

Filling in the Details: Skeleton Stories

Stories have beginnings, middles and ends. Often students can begin and end a story; much less often they can fill in the middle. The middle of a story is crucial. In mysteries, the middle contains twists, turns and clues. In the middle of romances, lovers make their major movements toward and away from each other. In horror and adventure stories, the middle is full of trials and tests, and functions as a sort of proving ground.

Shapelessness is a problem with most children's writing. The use of skeleton stories can give your students valuable experience with shape and form, with beginning, middle and end. Skeleton stories are like bones without flesh; they are merely plot lines. Nonetheless, they are stories, but stories at the simplest level. They have roughly the same relation to fiction as a coloring book does to art. Here is an example of a romance skeleton:

Boy meets girl. Boy and girl fall in love. Boy proposes, and girl accepts. Something happens to prevent their marriage. Boy and girl overcome the problem. Boy and girl marry.

25

A skeleton story raises questions. The answers to these questions serve as the flesh of the story: What do the girl and boy look like? How do they meet? How old are they? What prevents their marriage? Does the problem involve other characters, parents, a jealous suitor, an older sister?

Filling in the details should increase your students' writing ability and give them the experience of traveling through a complete story: beginning, middle and end. It is a landscape that must be traveled if they are to develop their writing skills. Our love of fiction is foremost our love of story. Unless the story grabs us, the form and style, even the philosophical content of a piece of writing, are likely to bore us.

Writing students of any age rarely sustain the energy, inspiration or confidence necessary to write a full story. But the advantages of completing a story are obvious. One gets a chance to see all the things that go into it, how the parts fit together, and why the end result moves our imaginations.

I try to make these skeletons as flexible as possible, generalized and loose with only enough direction to provide a student with minimal plot support, if he chooses to use it.

A crime is committed. (What? A kidnaping? Murder? Theft?) *It is discovered.* (How and by whom?) *Someone decides to try to solve the mystery.* (Who and why? For money? For love? Out of curiosity?) *The crime solver suspects certain people.* (Who? What are their backgrounds? Their relationship to the deceased, victim, or stolen object?) *The crime solver looks for clues.* (Where? Does she find any? What? What do the clues suggest?) *She follows suspects.* (Do they see her? What does she discover?) *Suddenly she finds herself in a dangerous position.* (Describe in detail. Is she caught? Is she hanging from a cliff? Stuck in an elevator in a burning building?) *She escapes, or gains control.* (How? In an elaborate way, in a simple way?) *She solves the mystery. The criminal confesses.* (What does he say?) *The mystery is solved.* (How does the mystery solver feel?)

Students need not follow the skeleton stories exactly.

26

They may, for example, begin at the end, after the mystery is solved, and tell the story in flashback. They may write it from the point of view of the criminal. They may omit elements, even the crime.

Skeleton stories need not be long:

> You were on your way to some place. You stopped at a well. You fell in. Luckily you caught the bucket rope. You are hanging on with one hand. You manage to feel your pockets and find two objects you believe can help you escape. You try to use them. What happens?

This skeleton story asks a question at the end, rather than making a statement. Fleshing it out, we would tell where the character was going, how she fell into the well, what she found in her pockets, and how she used what she found. The skeleton story doesn't disclose whether or not she escapes. That is left up to the writer.

It should be stressed when using the skeleton story that the writer must add details that are personal and original. This is the real work demanded by any story. The purpose of a skeleton story is to remove the pressure of having to create action by providing the writer with a ready-made plot structure. She should then be free to concentrate on other work, the meditative aspects of writing: creation of character, interaction, setting and perhaps even style.

Using Literature

Literature forms the basis for our work in genre. But how can we bring popular genre into our classrooms? I have a few suggestions to make. First, ask your class to read a popular book: Nancy Drew or a Hardy Boys mystery, for example. Then, discuss it seriously from whatever points of view you and your class find interesting. Often girls will stick as doggedly to Nancy as boys do to the Hardy Boys. Now and then try a switch. Suggest that the girls read the Hardy Boys and the boys read Nancy Drew. Pick a popular book like *While the Clock Ticked*, which half of the class is sure to have read anyway. I myself have used such books in class to discuss sexism, Oedipal theory and the notion of "good clean fun," and have also used them in discussions of characterization, plot and writing style. In college classes I have assigned books, or parts of books, such as *Jaws* and *Penmarric*. Older students were glad to read books that they would have chosen for themselves.

Another method of introducing popular literature is to bring in paragraphs and one-liners. Choose loaded or highly charged pieces of writing: "I kissed her. It was either that or slug her." "The gun against my neck went away and a white flame burned for an instant behind my eyes. I grunted and fell forward on my hands and knees and reached back quickly. . . . The jar of another on the head . . . and I made a hoarse sound." (Raymond Chandler's *The High Window*)

These bits should be short, powerful and evocative. Ask your students to try to see what is happening in a piece, or to add to it writing of their own. You might also ask, especially in a class with older students, for personal associations to such one-liners as "Go on. Beat it!"

In nearly every piece of fiction there will be at least a sentence or two devoted to the delineation of a character. Choose one such passage to present to your class. "His eyes were stone gray with flecks of cold light in them" (Chandler's *The Lady in the Lake*). "He wasn't the sort of man whose pocket you'd try to pick unless you had a lot of confidence in your fingers." "His eyes . . . looked as if they were hiding behind the watery film and under the bushy white brows only until the time came to jump out and grab something" (Dashiell Hammett's *Red Harvest*).

Sentences like these suggest personality through physical detail or psychological content. You know your class, so choose something on a level that they will easily relate to. Work with it by asking them to provide a fuller description, to give personal associations, to put the character in a new situation: what would he do if he was in a restaurant and ordered a hamburger but was served tunafish? What does his voice sound like? What does he look like? Ask your students to try to describe, in a charged or powerful way, someone in the class or someone they know.

So much of our response to literature is based on personal associations to one-liners. If this sort of experience can be had and discussed in your classroom, so much the better for your students. Charged bits of writing can be used to help them zero in on the experience. Encourage them to bring in their own favorite one-liners to share with their classmates.

29

The Recipes and How to Use Them

I like to think of the writing ideas in this book as recipes. Recipes in the hands of good cooks can always be improved upon. Throw in a little of this, a little of that, season to taste. But good writing recipes by themselves do not ensure good writing. Good teaching does the trick. A writing assignment is only as good as the teaching that precedes it. The teacher must set the mood from which valuable writing experiences come.

Recipes can come out tasting just like castor oil, too. "Oh no! Not another one!" It would be medicinal if the recipes in this book were mimeographed and passed out for your students to choose from once a week at Creative Writing Time or at Homework. The pleasure of writing stems from the feelings that are there before the writing begins, that are released during the writing, and then are shared afterward. The initial step of determining what to write, or "getting at the feelings," is essential. And for this, the teacher, not the recipe, is crucial.

Many questions have been built into each writing idea. Any or all of these may suggest to the teacher jumping-off places for discussion. You may also wish to ask your students to consider some of these questions while they are writing.

Not all the ideas are meant to produce writing with conventional beginnings, middles and ends. You will find that some pieces succeed because they are not wrapped up neatly in a bundle.

Choose the first genre you want to work with according to your own tastes, for the more appealing it is to you the easier and more pleasant it will be to teach. You can work with the less familiar genres later on.

The recipes, questions and examples are for *you* to use as *you* wish, to ignore or improve upon.

The Horror Story

The horror tale brings us to those crevices and dark places that most people visit in nightmares, dreadful fantasies and daydreams. The most familiar horror stories are those we experience in our life, or imagine experiencing. You are alone in your apartment or house. You hear noises. You imagine a thief. He finds you and murders you. Suddenly, you emerge from your ugly daydream. What could be bothering you, you wonder, to make you imagine such a dreadful thing? You are asleep, dreaming. Running from something awful, a giant rat or insect, a scarred man, a woman with a bloody face. You awaken, so frightened that you arouse the person sleeping peacefully next to you, or you turn on the light, or the radio—anything to bring you back to the reality of the safe and usual.

But we also imagine less exotic horrors: the dinner for important guests in which everything goes wrong. The job interview in which you are asked questions you don't know how to answer. A speech to a hostile audience that you can't even begin because you've forgotten every word of your memorized text. For a child, real-life horror may lie in the anticipation of a visit to the doctor's and the fear of unimaginable instruments or the terrifying needle.

Horror, then, may indeed be found in our everyday lives. A student will readily tell you "the most horrible thing that ever happened to me." Such stories will be about embarrassments, car accidents, physical injuries, etc. The word "horrible" has a clear and definite place in your students' vocabulary, and they have assigned to it many meanings and associations. I recommend drawing on these real-life experiences in discussion, as an introduction to the genre of horror. This approach has been effective with my young students as well as with my high school and college students.

As in the adventure story, the hero or heroine in a horror story engages in a test of wits and strength. However, the horror story foe is crueler, less reasonable and, in fact, often inhuman. He is unexplainable ("Where does he come from?") and uncontrollable. His unpredictability and immorality make him the most dangerous possible foe; he is not governed by human rules. For instance, unlike a monster, a human murderer does not usually eat his victim; he can be shot and killed with a gun. The hero of a horror story must somehow meet and conquer the superhuman horrible figure. In doing so he becomes its equal and then its superior. The process allows hero, reader, viewer and writer the great rush of omnipotence usually denied them in everyday life. In no other genre is this experience so extreme and so vivid.

Because you are pitting yourself against a supernatural power, in the horror story you must be that much closer to your divine capacity. The horror story hero must have the Right on his side. Whether or not he is clearly aided by God, or the Good, his personality and what he stands for are always righteous. The more horrible the horror, the stronger the human must be, and all the more shining his heroism.

A horror story may draw on our fear or our disgust. What

we fear does not always disgust us; it can awe and overwhelm us. Why does the disgusting frighten us? Because it suggests contagion; the victim may be turned into the horror figure, or catch its ugliness or sickness. The horror figure is a visual and tangible embodiment of our fears and anxieties. The creature is foreign, and we cannot place or identify it. Its alien features imply a power we do not understand and perhaps cannot control. It is not at all like us, and we cannot tolerate it for that reason. The term "monster" implies a deformed being who should never have been born.

Horrors come in all shapes and sizes. Some are human—like the maniacal murderer in *Psycho*; some are disgusting and grotesque in physical appearance, like a giant fly. Some have brute strength and an underdeveloped or warped intelligence, like Frankenstein's monster. There are those who attack any available victim, as a vampire does, and others like ghosts who wish to protect their homes from trespassers or to guard some valuable object. In any case, the pleasure in creating a horror figure comes most often from being able to control it, even to destroy it, or, very rarely, to coexist with it.

You might try to get your class in the mood for a horror project or writing idea through discussion. One question that has yielded good results for me is, "What is the most horrible thing you have ever experienced?" Anecdotes may be treated humorously or seriously. In the case of older students, stories may be drawn from any period of life. The teacher should tell a story about herself too. These stories may range from embarrassing to stomach-turning. Your students will probably, without any prodding, tell stories of strange things that have happened to them. Prepare for moving beds, dark shapes spreading along the wall, red moons, creaking noises in the hallway, etc. The heebie-jeebies may spread through your classroom.

Much of what they describe may take place at night or in the dark. Calling this to their attention is an excellent springboard for discussing fear, which is born out of what we cannot see and identify. Some black people have opposed the idea of identification of light with good and dark with bad, and this too may be a topic for discussion.

You might also ask your class whether all horror stories are disgusting. Why is the disgusting so frightening? Have you ever been disgusted? If not, what *would* disgust you? Frighten you? (For example, would being in an airplane crash, seeing limbs scattered all over, discovering an arm on your lap, disgust you? Frighten you? Both?) What is the difference between fear and disgust? Your students may have some real stories to tell. You might ask them to write two descriptions, the first to frighten the readers, the second to disgust them.

You may also wish to begin work on a horror project by reading to your class, or having your class read, a horror story. Particularly effective are Poe's "The Telltale Heart" and "The Black Cat." I'd also suggest some pseudo-documentaries on such phenomena as UFO's (unidentified flying objects), visitors from outer space, reincarnation, travel through time, mediums and mind reading; in short, stories drawn from purportedly true events that defy the laws of science. You can also try some science fiction.

The sense of wonder tinged with evil one gets from reading these stories is always an interesting point to discuss. Try to have students identify their feelings as clearly as they can. Explore the meaning of such remarks as "It makes me feel weird." "Strange" "weird" and similar words imply disorientation; the reader has been exposed to an unfamiliar world, a world that she doesn't understand, and that she is suspicious and afraid of.

Telling Horror Stories

Of the four genres, horror is probably the most immediately accessible and most easily understood. Students are rarely involved in full-scale mysteries, complete with victim, suspects and clues. Generally they have only a taste of a mystery—"Where did that sweater go?" Their adventures tend to be limited to school sports and relatively tame family outings—"Remember the time Daddy couldn't get the tent up and it began to rain?" Romances are seen on TV and in movies, and read in books, but these personal fantasies and experiences are rarely shared openly until adolescence.

But fear is an emotion we all know and talk about from an early age, when the world appears large and uncontrollable. (Although adventure, curiosity and love are also experienced from just as early an age, fewer stories are connected with these experiences.)

In no other genre are the telling of real experiences and the sharing of real stories so possible, or is memory so fertile, as they are in horror. When students begin to share stories that they have actually experienced, one association inevitably leads to another, and the stories really flow. Although children have inside them stories of love, adventure and mystery, stories involving fear seem to be the most *tellable*.

I'm not suggesting that children be encouraged to reveal their innermost fears, or that the stories they tell ought to be subject to psychological speculation. Nor, of course, are stories of fear or horror more worth telling than other kinds.

The stories need not be exotic, for by an early age students have lots of stories to tell from their own experiences. The horror stories I've heard had to do with ambiguous, mysterious events, sounds or images that have troubled them and that they have found no explanation for. Typical of this eminently sharable type of story is one told to me by a sixth-grader who remembered lying in bed late one night after everyone else in her family had gone to sleep. Suddenly she heard creaking noises and other inexplicable sounds in the corridor outside her room. She was convinced, and still is, that someone or something was outside her door. She was afraid to call for help because she thought that if she made noise the creature would realize she was alone in her room and would come in and hurt her. She lay motionless, silent and terrified.

A class experience in which such stories are told and shared can be helped along considerably if the teacher tells a story from her own experience. In one class where I was teaching as a visiting writer, the teacher told her story first, simply because she felt like it. It was a story from her childhood, and the students were as absorbed in trying to picture her as a child as they were in relating to the story itself.

My mother sent me out one cold November night to buy bread. We lived in the country, and there were no lights on the streets, as there are here in the city. I was about nine then. I remember looking up at the sky and seeing the moon. It looked like it was following me! It was so *dark* outside. I was really scared. I never bought that bread, because while I was walking I felt this thing rub against my shoulder. I was sure if I ran or screamed or did anything it would get me so I told myself to walk and look straight ahead, not to look up at the sky or in back of me or anything. Just to get home!

The children wanted to know what happened to her when she came home empty-handed and what she thought had scraped past her shoulder. "Oh," she said, "my mother understood, I guess. I don't really remember. Now that I think of it, it was probably only some low branch or bush that brushed against me. But I didn't know that then. From then on, for a real long time, I never went out at night alone."

I listened to this story, as absorbed as everyone else, and at the end of it I asked, "What did you imagine that terrible thing behind you looked like?" The teacher couldn't remember, but her students jumped at the chance to improvise their own garish visions: bald men with missing teeth and earrings, floating eyeballs, dismembered hands, slimy fishlike creatures, giant insects. Not all were described in clear physical detail, and sometimes I asked for a more evocative, detailed picture. The students seemed to enjoy the power their images had to make their classmates sigh or scream or laugh or close their eyes.

Some stories have to do with physical phenomena. As an example I will offer a story I told my students. One evening I was outside playing with friends when I looked up and for the first time saw an orange moon. Immediately I imagined that the moon was on fire. I thought there was some awful significance in my having been the first to spot this sight. Clearly, I was marked. I called my friends' attention to it. Together we noticed something else: the moon seemed to us to be revolving at a terrific rate. How else explain those changes in the pattern of its surface? We theorized about the end of the world and the approach of God, and wondered whether the moon was turning about the earth or whether, suddenly and spectacularly, we were turning about the moon. Baffled and frightened, we went to my mother, who as she sat on the stoop explained the illusion to us; clouds passing across the sky made the moon appear to be spinning.

It is no accident that all these stories take place at night. Night is our favorite time for bogymen, and we comfortably store all our imaginary creatures in its dark folds. This fact in itself makes for healthy and productive discussion, with many possible offshoots. Why does night make us feel so vulnerable? The closer we are to bedtime, the closer we are to being alone in the dark. At night our vision is limited. The less we actually see, the more we imagine and fear. The less we can predict, the more uncontrollable the world seems. Anything can happen in the dark. The infinite possibilities of darkness dwarf us and make us vulnerable.

Telling stories is different from writing them. Telling is immediate and personal. Often students are more willing to tell personal stories than to write them; telling takes less effort, and it gives students a chance to get closer to one another. I generally have my students sit in a circle, with lights off. One story begins and others follow freely, in an associative order, as one subject sparks the next. In a single morning, for example, stories can travel through bedtime fears, hurt animals, the moon, condemned buildings, haunted houses, ghosts and cemeteries.

Telling has a special power. Particularly telling true stories. It makes one a story teller. It is an ancient and satisfying form of expression. After all, man's first stories were *told*. The human voice holds us, transfixes us in its own special way. We tell stories all the time: "Guess what happened to me on the way to the supermarket," or "I was late because ..." Story telling is really one of the most basic and satisfying forms of entertainment. Yet it is done very rarely. It implies that we can entertain one another, and so ourselves. Everyone has stories: there is no lack of them. The

41

introduction of a topic is all that is needed to get the associative juices flowing.

Recipes for Horror

You are just beginning to turn into a werewolf. Changes occur in your body, and of course you begin to look different. (Hands and feet become paws, nose grows long, whiskers appear, ears turn pointed, skin grows fur, you begin to howl instead of talk, your whole being and way of thinking and feeling change from peace-loving to predatory and evil.) Describe in detail how each change (please add more to the above list!) comes over you and how it makes you feel physically and emotionally. You might want to write this in the form of a diary or scientific record. Or you may write it as a story. But work hard at imagining; for example, whiskers growing slowly but surely out of your cheeks, or the sensation of your nose growing long and then wet at the end. (Group imagining makes good class discussion.)

In hiding, you watch your friend, relative or acquaintance change from person to werewolf. How does the process look to you? How long does it take? Do you stay hidden or are you discovered?

Do research on wolves. Why do you think they are so readily portrayed as frightening and monstrous, so easily made into malevolent creatures? (They howl, they have yellow eyes that glow red at night, they travel in packs, etc.)

Research bats. Why are they so frightening to people? Write a monologue of someone who is terrified by bats and who sees or is pursued by a bat.

One may change not only into a wolf but into any animal or creature. But the transformation is a complicated process, with certain ceremonies and rituals attached to it. To begin with, a person may have to drink a special liquid or rub a special ointment on her skin. These concoctions must be made of hard-to-get things like sour milk, bats' wings, eagle eggs, secretions from a gnat's eye, a dragon's scale, froth from a mad dog, snake venom, etc. Second, the would-be werewolf or other creature probably must repeat a time-honored chant or prayer. The chant is followed or accompanied by explicit body movements: turning around twice, hopping on the left foot, pulling the hair, scratching the face, wringing the hands, etc. And of course, the ritual to promote transformation can only take place at certain times of the year, or month or day: The twenty-first of December in an odd year during a full moon; at midnight in thick fog; at sunrise, etc. Sometimes the ritual must be performed at a special location such as a swamp, the corner of 96th Street and Broadway, under a weeping willow tree in Connecticut, at the base of the Brooklyn Bridge, etc. *Write*: the entire ritual for transformation. Include the ingredients of the liquid or ointment, how to get them, how to prepare, mix and stir the concoction, how to drink or apply it. Also specify the accompanying body movements or dances, the time or season, and the place where the ritual must be held. (This activity can be taken on by the whole class as well as individually.)

A person who changes into a creature, or animal, also must change back again. In order to do so, he may have to duplicate the first ritual, or do something entirely different like jump into water, or drink a gallon of lamb's blood or bat's milk. Describe the rituals or acts through which a werewolf or other creature may return to human shape.

Through the ages people have devised methods for defending themselves against such creatures as werewolves and vampires. For example, crossing oneself, holding up a mirror, hitting the beast on the head three times with a silver knife, shooting it with silver bullets, blinking four times and saying a special prayer. (People don't necessarily defend themselves by killing the creature.)

Lycanthropy is a mental disorder in which a person thinks she is a wolf. A friend of yours has this disorder. (How did she develop it?) Write a dialogue in which you try to talk her out of her delusion. You may make this dialogue serious, silly or funny, but remember that your friend firmly believes she is a wolf who possesses all the characteristics wolves have (sharp teeth, keen sense of smell, wolf's howl) and that she will put up a good argument. Nevertheless, try to convince her if you can to return to the world of the human.

You are a hamrammer, a person who turns into whatever animal she eats. You have just sat down to dinner with your family. On the table may be duck, chicken, beef, fish, deer or elephant. After your first few bites you turn into the animal you have just consumed. Right there in front of your family! What do they do?

The ilimu is an animal that eats people and, after having eaten one of them, turns into a person. As a person, the ilimu keeps on eating people. Write a story about such a creature. You might want to let the ilimu describe how it eats and changes into a person. Once it has become a person, how does the ilimu snare its human victims? What does an ilimu look like, before and after?

The walls of your room suddenly:
    —start closing in on you
    —turn into sheets of ice
    —turn into waves of water about to crash down on you
and drown you
    —turn hairy and furry like a living creature
    —turn into the insides of a whale
Unfortunately, you cannot escape your room. What happens?

You are walking down the street. You notice a hearse go by. Something compels you to follow it. You must! You attend the funeral. Suddenly you realize that it is _____ who has died!

You are in a room with lots of people. You start talking to them, one after another, but they pay no attention to you. You realize, slowly and horribly, that they cannot see you. You are invisible!

You have been invited to a party. The written invitation includes the address where the party is to be held. It also promises that all your friends will be there. In fact, the party is in your honor. The address seems quite out of the way. You travel a long time to a very remote place. Finally you arrive at the destination, a large mansion with many fine rooms. You let yourself into the house and discover that you are the only one in the place. No one else arrives. Who has sent you here and why?

You are a homunculus, made by a scientist in a laboratory. You are only six inches tall, and the scientist who made you keeps you in a bottle. Do you remember being "born"? (You were born fully grown.) How did the spark of life feel as it traveled through your body? What is your relationship to the scientist? How does she treat you? One day you find that another bottle has been placed next to yours. Inside is another homunculus just like you! You get her attention. Is she a stranger or someone you know? What do you talk about? Does the scientist let you out of your bottle to visit or does she keep the two of you apart? What finally happens?

You are ageless. You cannot grow older. You remain the same age always. You are good-looking, never wrinkle, never show signs of aging, never die. You see your friends and relatives die. What is life like for you? You might write a lament, a confession, an autobiography. How did you come to be ageless? (A curse? A pact with the Devil?)

You are a somnambulist, a sleepwalker. You aren't aware of what you're doing while you are sleepwalking. Where do you go and what happens? Often sleepwalkers go to the same place and do the same thing every night. They are reliving some personal drama, or acting out an event that they wish would happen. Why do you sleepwalk? What is the significance of your actions?

You are hypnotized by a mad doctor. (What in the world made you go to him in the first place?) You are at his command. What are some of the things he has you do? What happens? Do you rebel? If so, how? How does it feel to be hypnotized? To fall under a spell? To do things while you are hypnotized? (How are your actions when you are hypnotized different from your actions when you are fully conscious?)

You have made a pact with the Devil. He has agreed to give

you something you want, in return for your soul. (What is it you want? Money? Fame? A red convertible? A new fur coat? A sister? Strength?) You might really think about what you would want in real life if you could somehow have it. You might write a two-act dialogue or play, the first act depicting you making the agreement with the Devil and the second showing the Devil returning to collect your soul. What happens when a soul is collected? You might write the monologue of a soul that has been promised or delivered to the Devil. What kinds of things would you do with your special power?

A zombie is a dead person who is removed from his grave and then through magic and sorcery seems to come back to life. He does everything a living person does, but he is stiff, rigid, like a machine or robot. You have been observing someone for a while (a friend, a boss, neighbor, relative, etc.). Something just isn't right with him. He seems unreal. He talks strangely, never blinks, doesn't appear to breathe. (What other qualities of a zombie would show how unreal he was?) He doesn't look at you when he talks; his eyes are dead. One day you realize that he is a zombie! (How do you discover this? Do you find him killing someone, or doing something very sinister or talking to someone suspicious who seems to have control over him?) Zombies are controlled by unscrupulous living people. Zombies themselves do not know they are dead. If you want to remind a zombie that he is dead, and send him back to the grave, you must feed him meat with salt. What happens to you when you make your discovery? Does the controller of the zombie find out that you know? What does he do? You might also try a dialogue with a zombie (this is an excellent writing assignment, popular and fun). Remember, no matter what you say to a zombie, he does not respond emotionally, or humanly.

Describe the four different faces of a sea monster, a space creature, robot, a zombie. (If you like this, you may also wish to go on and describe their bodies: hands, feet, trunk, skin, hair, etc.)

A family can be cursed because of a sin or wrongdoing committed by a family ancestor. The victim of the wrongdoing curses the perpetrator and all the children of future generations in that family. Tell the history of a cursed family. When did the ancestor live? What grievous act did he or she commit? Who cursed the family? Put this curse into words. What can be done to change, undo or end it? (The attempt is usually made by a brave person.) A family curse causes great unhappiness: divorces, blindness, serious illness, insanity, early deaths, suicides, murders, etc.

Places can be cursed too. No person can go to an accursed place without suffering dire consequences: death, disappearance, madness, loss of speech, paralysis, etc. Sometimes the place (a tomb, castle, part of a forest, a condemned building, your own apartment) contains something horrible and ugly. When the visitor sees this ugly thing, he is somehow adversely affected by it. Describe an accursed place. Have yourself, or a character, visit this place. What physical and emotional changes occur? Describe in detail. How did the place become accursed? (Usually something terrible has happened there, or someone may have put a curse on it.) Describe the aura of an accursed place.

You are a sailor on a phantom boat, doomed to sail the seas for the rest of eternity, going nowhere, sometimes approaching land but never being able to set anchor. What is your life like on this boat? Suppose that one day someone in a small sailboat approached you and started to talk to you?

A ghost is doomed to wander throughout eternity, without rest. In life she alienated man or God. She may wander over familiar territory, through the castle or house or fields that once were hers. Or she may, especially if she died violently, constantly return to the scene of her death. A ghost usually haunts a place because she is reliving her past. Tell the story of a wandering ghost. How did she die? Why must she wander? Where does she go? How does it feel never to sit or sleep or rest? What happens when people see her? Does she do something special when she haunts (scream an oath, lie on a bed next to a human, chase a man ax in hand)?

Write the curse uttered by a dying, bitter woman. Why is she bitter? Whom or what is she cursing? (Curses may be very specific. For instance, one might curse the third son of a third son.)

Write a blessing.

Describe an evil eye.

You are a magician casting a spell. First, you must prepare your magic concoction. What kinds of things do you toss into your caldron? What do you say over the concoction before you drink it? What special movements or gestures do you make?

Amulets and talismans are objects, natural or man-made, that possess magic or divine power. Did you ever have a lucky piece that brought you special good fortune and that you carried with you on certain occasions? Go outside and try to find something you would consider a good-luck piece. What criteria do you use in selecting one?

Second sight and skin sight (both have been scientifically documented) occur when people although blind, can see things as though they had eyes in back of their head, or can perceive colors with only their hands and fingers. Write a story about a person who has such gifts. (Does the gift ever help her? Hurt her? Get in her way? How did she discover she had it? Do people believe that she has it?)

Spirits have stories. They tell of their lives and their deaths, and of their lives after death. Spirits are the souls, or ghosts, of dead people who return to speak to the living. A seance is held by a spiritualist who supposedly makes contact with this living soul. She may imitate the spirit's voice, or she may call the spirit forth to rap or knock on a table or wall with signals that mean yes and no. If the spirit speaks through the spiritualist, she can say anything; she can talk. But if the spirit raps, then she can answer only yes or no. Two raps mean yes. Silence means no. The spiritualist, usually hired by the dead person's friends or relatives, asks the spirit questions about her life, death, disappearance, some mystery connected with her death, etc. Students may prepare, individually or in groups, stories about a spirit. The class may ask questions of the group or individual, and try to find out as much as they can about the spirit. The student spiritualist may answer yes or no by rapping, or the spirit may speak directly through one of the people in the group.

What do you think happens to people after they die?

Some Egyptian noblemen were buried with living servants who were supposedly going to serve them in the other world. You are a servant of a nobleman. One day he dies. You anticipate being locked up in an airless, dark, windowless tomb. How do you feel when you learn the nobleman has died? Describe his funeral ceremony. (Is there a procession? A sacrifice? A priest? Singing?) What is it like to be locked in that tomb? What do you see around you before the door is finally closed? What is it like to be in a room with a mummy?

Design a tomb. A tomb has many rooms, rooms that are reproductions of the rooms the dead person had when he was alive, rooms for worship, rooms for sleeping, eating, a kitchen, etc. Draw a plan for a tomb (aerial view), including its furnishings. The Egyptians decorated the walls of their tombs with writing or drawings depicting events from the dead persons' lives. Draw a wall that might represent your own life.

What is the most horrible experience you ever had? The most horrible you ever heard of?

What is the most disgusting experience you ever had? Heard of?

Describe the ugliest, most frightening face you can imagine.

Prepare a disgusting menu to be eaten perhaps by monsters, creatures, witches, or your enemies.

You are hiking in a swampy forest area. Suddenly you see something rising up from the swamp. You try to run, but the ground beneath you is wet and soggy and slows you down. What is coming at you from the swamp? What does it look like? Does it make noise? Can you draw a picture of it? How is a swamp monster different in appearance from other kinds of monsters? (Since it is born of the swamp, it may resemble a swamp.) What happens?

What does a ghost's voice sound like?

Write the monologue of a mad scientist about to perform an evil operation. (What's the operation? How does a mad or crazy person talk?)

Make a list of screams. Then scream them. (*Agggh!* You son of a rotten creep! *EEEEEEEEEEEEEEEE*! Get *out* of here!!! Keep away!)

The cave men practiced sympathetic magic. If a cave man wished a certain thing to happen, like rain or a successful buffalo hunt, he would draw pictures of a rainstorm or a buffalo hunt on the walls of a cave. (This cave was often used only for sympathetic drawings, which were painted or etched onto the walls.) In your own life, consider some things you would like to have happen. Try to represent them in a drawing or painting. Approach the drawing with the belief that what you draw will really happen. Perhaps the cave men performed a ceremony before making their drawings, to dispose the gods to grant them what they wanted. Get your students to write and enact such a ceremony. (The teacher should try to create a mood of belief. Turn off the lights, play percussion music, do whatever you think will help to create a primitive, magic mood.) Drawings or paintings do *not* have to have a clear or representational meaning to anyone but the painter, who can explain her work after everyone has finished.

Some magicians belonged to sects that required them to perform certain daily rituals in order to maintain their power. They might blink twice upon waking, put their right shoe on first, sprinkle their sheets with special water after rising from bed, wash their face with their right hand only, etc. Prepare a ritual that can be performed as a daily task. It should consist of ordinary things that one does every day. But these things must be performed in a special manner, for example brushing the hair with the right hand only and brushing exactly 46 strokes.

Prepare a ritual or ceremony by which a person becomes a witch.

You are a royal inquisitor. Your job is to protect the country from witches. In a sense you are like a prosecutor. Interrogate a witch. Ask questions like: Do you pray to the moon? Do you own a crystal ball? Present prepared statements by witnesses who claim to have seen the accused involved in witchcraft or sorcery. If you do not wish to write as a lawyer would, just write an accusation in which you accuse the person of being a witch. Even an accusation, however, must offer some evidence of witchlike behavior.

You are accused of witchcraft; respond to this accusation. You are not a witch; deny the accusation. You *are* a witch; you are powerful!

The Adventure Story

In an adventure one tests one's strength and wits against an awesome opponent. The opponent may be natural, human or superhuman, but he is usually less demoniacal than the villain in a horror story. His power and strength are limited by earthly rules. The hero is motivated by a desire or need to reach a certain goal. He may be seeking a person (whom he is trying to rescue or to kill), a place (the top of a mountain, the ocean floor), or a thing (a priceless jewel or coin).

The hero moves toward his goal while an opposing force places obstacles in his path. The hero encounters and must overcome falling rocks, landslides, floods, a gang of desperados, a sensitive alarm system, etc.

Although fear is seldom an overt element in adventure, the hero does admit awe of the opposition. He looks the enemy square in the eye and says, "You're bigger than I" and then tackles it anyway. He is realistic and courageous. He is not, as he is in the horror story, necessarily on the side of God. Readers and viewers identify with him not because of his goodness but because he has *purpose*. He earns our respect because he puts his life on the line, for an idea, for a person, or even out of self-interest. Of all the genre heroes the heroes of mysteries and adventures are the most idealistic. Both pursue the truth: the detective tries to find out what really happened, while the adventurer attempts to live without compromise. More than any other genre hero, the adventurer tries to achieve a harmony between the way he wants to live and the way he does live. His being true to himself is often what leads him into adventure. The adventurer is also concerned with the discrepancy between what he has and what he should have. He tries to get what is rightfully his, or tries to assume again his rightful place.

The adventure hero is resourceful, strong and intuitive. He knows how to turn to his own advantage the very forces opposing him. He digs a hole in the snow and curls up inside, letting the snow, by all rights his enemy, protect him from the cold. He also demonstrates physical stamina and endurance. Shot through the leg, he makes it to cover and continues to fire back at his enemy. The sole survivor of a shipwreck keeps his raft afloat against the assault of storms and waves.

The hero possesses a special sensitivity that allows him to outguess his opponent. This peculiar ability suggests the relatedness of the antagonists. Because he knows him so well, physically and psychologically, he can always put himself in his opponent's shoes and correctly predict what he is going to do. The hero leaps out of the way of a falling rock, avoids an exploding mine, reaches shelter moments before a downpour. This sixth sense always saves him in the nick of time.

Domination and superiority are themes of the adventure story. The cowboy hero rides into a town ruled by a band of cutthroats. The cowboy takes them on and ultimately wins the allegiance of the town (and a sheriff's badge). An airplane pilot is threatened when a sudden storm erupts, and his plane is in serious danger of crashing. In both adventures, the opposing force is chaotic and destructive. The hero feels obligated to put things right, to impose order on chaos.

An adventure is the dramatization of a test. Every person has undergone tests during his life. Watch a very young child hop on one foot for as long as he can just to prove his capability and strength. Or a grown woman ask her boss for a raise. Like the adventure hero, the child and the woman ask themselves, "Can I do it?" Your students' tests may include fistfights, riding a bike without hands, running a race, trying to solve a math problem.

The wish for adventure probably begins as soon as the child crawls, as soon as he begins to move away from the watchful eye of his mother. The craving for adventure is stimulated by the urge for growth. We move away from the familiar to confront the unknown and difficult. The larger, more threatening world gives us a chance to prove our resourcefulness.

An adventure may begin in any setting or situation. Essentially it is the story of a journey. One gets to one's destination involuntarily or entirely through one's own efforts. One may get lost and wander into a precarious situation. One may be exploring. Ultimately, most adventurers want to return home.

Here are a few basic adventure-story types, all involving the idea of a journey:

The Kidnap. A woman is taken by surprise, against her will, to a place she has never been before. She may not know why she has been taken. She struggles against her captors, and adventures occur while she is trying to escape. If she doesn't know who kidnaped her or why, she usually finds this out, with other secrets she is not supposed to know. Possessing these secrets, she becomes even more of a threat to her captors and is guarded more closely, or hunted more intensely if she has escaped. In addition to getting back home, she now tries to turn the tables on her enemies.

Getting Back. Although the return home is always a part

of an adventure story, it may provide the entire framework for an adventure. Homer's *Odyssey* is the prime example.

The Journey to Discovery. The hero sets out to find a person, place or object that holds some particular meaning or importance—religious, personal or strategic (as in a war adventure). Opposing forces stand in his way. Often the hero is led off course by the maneuverings of rivals or enemies. He finds himself in alien, unfamiliar territory and tries to get back to the point where he began his search. His reward for ultimately finding the object of his search is usually personal satisfaction, but sometimes it is money. Many adventures end with the hero gaining a beloved. She is usually physically weak but loyal, and she possesses a core of emotional strength. One reward for brave and great action, then, is often a love object.

Transformation. The hero finds himself transformed. For example, he suddenly becomes a cockroach, and things that were once benign or of no consequence—other insects, mice and cats—suddenly threaten his life.

The Wolf Boy. The hero as a baby or young child is kidnaped, or is left or wanders by accident into the forest or jungle, into a primitive environment where animals reign. Wolves, monkeys or other animals adopt the child and rear him according to animal law. His adventures involve first understanding and then adapting to animal or tribal law and confronting those animals who transgress this code. At some point when the hero is older, he usually comes again into contact with humans, and often finally decides to re-enter human society because he believes he belongs there or feels a need for or attraction to women.

Exploration. The hero sets out to explore an unknown territory for pleasure or for gain. He may be planning to draw a map of it or to master it, as in the case of mountain climbing. His adventures usually test his resourcefulness. The environment itself, and sometimes competitors or natives of the area, are his enemies. Elements of an exploration story include: anticipation of the journey, making preparations, traveling to the new territory, landing at one's destination, exploration, discovery of new things, attainment of a goal. Along the way, of course, the hero is periodically thwarted.

Man Against the Elements. In order to gain his goal, the hero must fight to stay alive. He battles sun, wind, rain, rivers, deserts, sand, snow, cold, etc. As in the story of exploration, the hero must prove his resourcefulness and stamina.

An adventure story is suspenseful. The reader alternates between fear and relief as passengers squirm out of sinking ships, heroines pull themselves up the sides of cliffs, swimmers struggle to the shore after having endured the sea for days. We want to know what happens next, and *how* it happens. We like to compare what we might have done in a similar situation with what the characters do. In our heart we know the hero will make it, but there's always that chance that he won't. . . .

Uncertainty and anxiety are everyday experiences for most of us, so why should their dramatization please us so? Probably because the hero never fails to overcome them. His judgment and intuition always prevail. He can keep embarking on adventures because he is confident in himself and is not afraid of what will happen to him if he takes a chance. He makes *us* anxious, but he is too secure to be paralyzed by anxiety himself. This is the source of our greatest attraction to the adventure story: although we are held in suspense we know that in the end we will be satisfactorily delivered from it.

In the adventure story, the emphasis is on action. We know the hero by the kind of action he takes. Does he rush into things? Plan first? Does his resourcefulness come from books he has read or from past experience? The hero's cool capability impresses the reader over and over again.

In an adventure the hero does not meditate on the beauty of the hills: he climbs them. He does not ponder on the blinding snow storm: he drives his truck through it. The emphasis on physical action leads to details of movement; to precise rather than poetic description.

An adventure gives the reader a chance to escape from reality and participate vicariously in a highly active fantasy. A good deal of this fantasy has to do with destruction, for the hero constantly comes into contact with obstructive or destructive forces. He must fight back. Pitted against murderers, thieves, and overwhelming natural forces, he must keep from getting destroyed. So he is always escaping serious injury or death.

We identify with the hero of an adventure story. It is through him that we experience the adventure. He advances the story by successfully passing each test that stands in the way of his completing the journey and attaining his goal. His attainment of the goal gives us our satisfaction: that pleasure we look forward to when we begin reading an adventure story.

Matthew's 'Survival'

Matthew was above average height and weight, sturdy and well built. Because of his size and strength he was often given positions of responsibility in school, such as that of hallway monitor. He had a quick temper and expressed his anger vehemently, but verbally; rarely did he have to resort to physical force. He was no bully, but he did come down hard on anyone who tried to hand him "a line of bullshit." His peers regarded him with respect and admiration.

He had an almost studied, professional earnestness about him that he displayed in front of adults whom he particularly wanted to take him seriously. Sophisticated beyond his years, he was intent on proving himself capable in an adult world. When he was in an anxious mood, he appeared to be bearing the weight of the world on his shoulders. No one could bring him out of such a mood. He worried about tests, visits to the dentist, family matters. He worried about the same things all children worry about, but the worry seemed to affect him more deeply, to capture him and hold him.

Although he was extremely loyal, physically defending friends or helping them with homework and school work, he could also be aloof and seemed to enjoy, even crave, an occasional bout of melancholy. He would set himself apart from his friends, letting them fade into the background of his life for a while. He would ignore them or tell them to shut up because he had work to do or something important to think about.

Matthew was introduced to all four genres. He wrote interestingly in each, but remarkably well in adventure.

The demands of the genre paralleled the demands Matthew made on himself. He spent eight months—a long period of time to sustain interest—completing an adventure novel. This novel, *Survival!*, is about some army and civilian workers on a mission to bring aid and relief to a starving Indian town. On the way, their plane crashes. To stay alive, the survivors of the crash must try to band together as equals.

Through this story Matthew represented and expressed important facets of himself: his keen understanding of power and his need to win, to survive tests, to use his strength and cleverness. A moral tone is evident throughout. He expresses impatience and annoyance with the stupidity and fear he perceives in other people. (Matthew could be very critical at times.) He describes loneliness and depression so well that we know he has had these feelings himself. His characters are individualized and independent, and their interplay with one another creates real dramatic tension. At age twelve, Matthew is a writer. His prose style is a lot like his speech: tough and abrupt, it pushes us around.

Matthew depicts a power play in the following scene, which is set before the plane takes off:

Major John H. Danbury took a cigarette out of his pocket and stuck it loosely in his mouth. He turned his swivel chair towards his friend, Lieut. William B. Starr, and dangled the cigarette loosely from his mouth in front of Lieut. Starr's face. Lieut. Starr looked at his friend, completely unaware of what the cigarette meant. Suddenly something snapped inside of him. He quickly took out a lighter from his pocket and opened the top, and a flame came out and lit up the major's cigarette.

"You'll learn sooner or later," the major joked.

Although the survivors must "come together as allies helping one another [because] that is the key to survival," Matthew's novel explores what happens when two people act selfishly and leave the group. Mrs. Bronson, a religious fanatic, flees in terror. Chapter 4, "The Ordeal of Jane Bronson," describes the outcome of Dave's and Rob Gunn's search to find her and bring her back:

> "Jane, are you there?" Dave shouted.
>
> Suddenly there was a loud rumble, and then a silence. They were stunned for a brief moment, and then they realized something happened. They ran to see what it was. When they got there, all they saw was a big pile of rocks, and they also saw some kind of a liquidy thing.
>
> They ran toward the rock pile, desperately hoping to find Jane Bronson. They started to lift rocks from the pile when Dave stepped in some kind of liquid. He looked down into the puddle and screeched, "Blood! Blood! Jane's blood!"
>
> "Help me get her out of the pile," Rob said.
>
> Dave said one thing and fainted, "My God."
>
> "Oh, damn, what's the matter?" Rob lifted his brother and slapped him on the face. His brother came to and recovered quickly.
>
> They began to lift Jane out of the rocks when a bear came out of the rocks in front of them!!!
>
> "My God!" yelled Dave.
>
> "Dave, don't move a muscle, stand perfectly still," Rob said through the side of his mouth.
>
> Dave trembled with fear. He was completely bewildered. He asked himself, "Why stand still? What if the bear attacked?" But he had confidence in his brother, so he did not move. But he couldn't stay still forever, and he was becoming restless.

Rob knew what he had to do in this situation, for he had been on camping expeditions before and had encountered bears numerously.

Dave was scared. He was nervous, and his tenseness grew and grew. He couldn't take it, he had to move. He suddenly sneezed!

The bear jumped in fright and swung around. He roared a loud furious roar. His white teeth glistened in the light of the flashlight.

Dave started to run. Rob took the knife from the sheath hanging on his belt. The bear came after Dave, who couldn't run much longer. Rob came in front of the bear and dove at him, thrusting the knife in the beast's collarbone.

This time when the bear roared it sounded like a high pitched screech. The bear stumbled many times but managed to stay on his feet. Blood was coming out the animal's body, like sap coming out of a tree. The knife apparently had found its way into the chest muscles of the huge monster. This was one spot in an animal's body where death comes the easiest. His whole body turned juicy red. He finally fell to the ground and died instantly.

Dave was unharmed. "Rob, are you okay?" Dave asked his brother.

Rob leaned over the carcass of the bear. "Yes, I'm okay."

Matthew describes the futility of his character's situation as Major Danbury tries to fight a faceless enemy and then meditates on the hopeless landscape.

The major had the first watch that night. All seemed quiet for awhile. Suddenly something moved in the bushes, about five or six feet away from where Major Danbury was sitting, or daydreaming. He heard it, despite his daydreaming. He swung quickly around and started toward the spot, knife in hand. He came to the bushes and cautiously rushed an opening in the bush. All of a sudden something jumped out of the bushes and sent the major hurtling backwards. He fell on his back and the knife came hurtling down toward the major's face. The major, recovering from his fall, rolled over and avoided the knife by about an inch. He turned around and looked around to see what had jumped at him. He saw absolutely nothing but the dense darkness of the spring night.

In these parts spring seemed like winter, summer like autumn, and winter, well, winter here is just another story. Winter was bitter cold, food was scarce, and life was almost impossible. Even the native animals of these mountains died because of no food, or because of the fact that the bitterness of the cold was too much for them.

Major Danbury got up and pulled the knife from the ground. He searched the dark mountainous terrain, expecting to find something, but he didn't.

Rob Gunn devises a plot of his own to save the group of survivors. He shows the intense resolve that later leads to his death.

Rob paced up and down along the muddy ground. He thought very carefully about the cliff, about being rescued, about dying. It was all very clear to him, now, death, being rescued, and especially the cliff. The cliff, he thought, is our only hope of being rescued. . . .

Rob walked over to the cliff, almost rubbing against it. "It's either you or me," he said, slapping his hand against the moist rocky surface. He raised a leg and slipped it into a little crevice in the rock. Then he lifted his arm and put it into a crevice, and pulled himself up. The major suddenly appeared below.

"What are you doing?" he snapped at Rob.

Rob did not answer. The major started to climb after Rob. When he reached Rob's feet he grabbed them, trying to pull him down. Rob pulled up his leg, and with fantastic strength he pushed his leg down and hit the major's chin. This resulted in the major's head jerking backward. He landed on a pointed rock. He landed on his back and the pointed rock shot up through his back, coming through his stomach.

When Rob looked down he was so terrified with what he saw, he accidentally let go. He also fell, doing several somersaults. His arm hit the pointed rock, tearing the flesh so badly that his arm, upon hitting the ground, separated from his shoulder socket. Blood flowed unstoppingly from both their bodies.

"Sonuva . . ." The major's supposed last words trailed off into sleep, a sleep that would last forever.

Just before they are rescued, Lieutenant Starr, the last surviving hero, faces feelings of loneliness:

> The lieutenant now sat in front of the crackling fire, smoking a Camel Cigarette. His shirt was unbuttoned, and the wind blew his dark, stringy hair in all directions. He felt lonely, strangely enough, and he wanted company. He was depressed.
> Suddenly the tremendous roar of a motor deafened him. The cigarette dropped to the ground. Lights flashed in all directions, voices were shouting, people were scattered all around.
> Then in all the excitement the stunned lieutenant managed to get some words out of his mouth. "Over here!!" he shouted at the top of his lungs.

Matthew's self shines out through his novel. It is a clear and excellent example of the variety and scope of a student's emotions as expressed through genre. Matthew felt naturally inclined toward adventure. It suited his feelings, temperament and disposition. I once asked him why he had less success with and interest in mysteries, horror stories and romances. It was a hard question for him to answer. He thought for a while and began a lot of sentences that he couldn't complete. "I guess I can't write them," he finally said, "because I just don't think that way."

Like Matthew, some students show predilections for specific genres. If they begin an adventure story, they wind up writing a romance! One of my students when asked to write a romance couldn't keep himself from describing a very elaborate and exciting airplane hijacking. But, he explained to me later, there *was* a honeymooning couple in the airplane. Students should be introduced to all genres but never forced to write in any one. If interestingly presented, however, other genres will be absorbed even by seemingly inattentive students. Don't worry if a student cannot or does not write in all genres. Any creative imagination will prefer one type of story over another; if given the chance, a student like Matthew will express his preference.

'The Sailboat'

It was an old wooden affair with hand-sewn sails, hand-carved masts. One sailed her by the mainsail, and not, like present-day boats, by the jib. There was something charming about its wooden body. Dark green on the outside, banana yellow inside. A real nautical lady with dignity and grace. I decided to take her out alone. I had had some sailing experience, enough, at least, to round one bend of the shoreline. I contemplated doing more. Tacking a sandwich— but, no. I was better off just rounding that next bend. It was early evening and I was not the adventurous sort. A taste would do.

I rigged up her mainsail and the freeloading jib that never really earned its keep and that like me was only out for the ride.

I was ankle deep in cold sea water. I checked the mainsail. Not a ripple. I could stayed moored for a while and bail. The entrepreneur who rented us the boat had sworn to my husband and me that her wood would "seize up" in a matter of two or three days. That had been over two weeks ago and I had just emptied her of sixteen gallons.

I freed us from the buoy and off we were. Just her and me. But there was no wind. The sail was as smooth as the sheet on an army cot. Yet we were moving! And not so slowly either. But the sails? Not a luff. Not even a whiffle.

Goodbye, house. Who needed a sail? The current had taken me where I had planned on going, but not in the manner I had planned, nor at the speed.

Oars, get moving! Commando Karen at the helm. Okay, you swabbies, sink or swim, this is it.

I could drown. Or worse, fall in the water. That icy cold was more effective than Novocaine. The boat was filling up around my ankles again. I worriedly watched my life jacket slosh around under the seats in the stern. If I stopped rowing to put on the jacket, I'd lose whatever ground I'd made in the last ten minutes. I was moving further out than seemed safe. The current would take me out to sea if I didn't work harder.

Row left. Row right. Row left. Row right. I'd lick this thing. I'd get back home. I was determined. Clenched teeth, knees outstretched, body arched back to catch the heft of the stroke, arms in time, hands gripped tight around the oar. Good hard long strokes. Good hard long . . .

Crack.

It was a crack and it sounded like a crack. *Crack.* Like that. And what had cracked? Why, my oarlock, of course. Without it there was no way of attaching my oar to the boat so that I could row.

I couldn't believe it. A disaster was actually happening to *me.* An ordinary person. Now that I wasn't rowing, the shoreline was traveling by at a faster rate than ever.

Newspaper headlines, all right maybe just an article in the Bangor *News*, a slight mention in the *Times*. How could it happen to me? It couldn't happen to me. A cheerleader. I had the spirit and the baton. I was going to reach that shore in this boat, come hell or high water. Now, that was apt. I had nothing to do but row like a cheerleader and talk to myself for the next twenty minutes.

The shore grew closer. The sky was turning gray unexpectedly fast. The ocean was turning wilder. This was no night to be out alone.

I threw my anchor onto shore. The waves threw the boat against the jagged rocks. I stood up to undo the sails, in case a wind should come up—but that was ridiculous. Nevertheless, my sailing manual always recommended taking the sails down in uncomfortable situations.

She couldn't take the next wave and neither could I. We both toppled sideways into the water, she righting herself a little faster than I did. I hung onto the side of the boat and pulled myself onto the rocks with my legs.

I let out the anchor line and the boat drifted farther out, away from the harmful rocks. I secured the anchor.

Now what? What had I thought that reaching shore would accomplish, since this shore was a half a mile from my haul off? I decided to try to pull the boat around the coastline to my house. The waves crashed against the rocks, the boat swerved from side to side as I pulled it around the shore by its anchor and rope. Cold and wet did not exist for me. I was something out of *The African Queen*.

That was okay for Katharine Hepburn, but for me it was ridiculous. I wasn't going very far and the boat was getting stuck in between rocks in the shallow water.

You can't pull this boat back home.

But . . .

You can't, I interrupted.

But how to find help? I didn't know where the nearest house was. And what help would I find even if I found some? What could anyone do for me? Feed me, dry me, be nice. But who could offer me a dock on a coast where there were no docks, or the right-size oarlock? There was no use staying here. It had grown darker. Fog was beginning to move in and nobody in her right mind was going to happen by to lend a

71

hand.

I'd have to let the boat out on more line, secure the anchor with more rocks and set out into the forest. If I was lucky, which hardly seemed likely, the moon might be bright even through the clouds and fog so that I could see where I was walking.

Walking? I had no shoes. They had toppled over into the water when the boat tipped. I was barefoot! I thought of the Indians who walk over broiling coals: well, they do it. Barnacles, sharp-edged rocks. I added this to the images of broken glass and rusty tin cans, everything I'd been warned about when walking barefoot. But you're not on Coney Island, I had to remind myself, or in Central Park.

The woods were perfectly still. I could hear the waves breaking against the shore, the foghorn, the gulls. Yet all around me the forest was motionless. It was another world.

Smack up against a dead tree trunk. Did that hurt! I nursed my toe. I practically wanted to double up and stick it in my mouth, it hurt so bad. Fantasies of having walked on poison ivy stopped me.

I was surrounded by enemies. Mother Nature was supposed to be kind and wonderful, yet here she was, murdering me, threatening me with poison ivy, porcupines, unfamiliar sounds, moose droppings.

In the distance I saw a slab of white. The actual physical part of my walk had demanded so much of my concentration that for a second I'd forgotten what I had been looking for. It seemed to be the side of a house, as I walked closer. Suppose there was no one home? Suppose there was someone home? Out here in the Maine woods privacy was sacred. I imagined the numerous domestic scenes I might interrupt. A family sitting down to eat, an old man washing dishes, a young couple walking around their house without clothes.

But I found no people. Nor did I find a home. It was a boathouse. It had no windows. I walked around it looking for the front door but instead of a door I found the entire wall of the boathouse open, facing onto the ocean. The structure was hidden so well by the trees that I had not seen it from the shore. Yet, from the boathouse, I could see a long and beautiful view of the ocean.

The sun was an orange glow, sinking below the silhouettes of the neighboring islands off the coast. The fog rolled in gently. A few clouds rolled past the moon. It was a scene I'd witnessed from my porch many times. Ordinarily it made me feel serene, harmonious. But tonight the sunset and fog only worried me, made me feel insecure and at its mercy.

Inside the boathouse were rowboats, canoes, buoys, lobster traps, pulleys, nets; off in the corner were six pairs of oars leaning one pair against the next. Out of my pocket I took the broken stem of the oarlock and measured it against those oars fastened with locks. I found one just a fraction thicker. Would it fit my boat?

As soon as I had made up my mind to take it, it occurred to me that I was stealing. What if someone caught me? But of course they would understand my predicament. But suppose they didn't? I stepped outside the bathhouse. Printed above me I read: *PROPERTY OF DANA*

I had met him once at a party. He seemed to like political conversation best and swayed everyone he spoke to in that direction. *NO TRESPASSING*. He was a staunch conservative whose credo was self-sufficiency. Explain an oar theft to a man who'd have me swim home with the boat roped to my waist? He spent his days at the boathouse, I knew, playing solitaire, looking out onto the ocean, sipping iced tea and eating cookies, surrounded by all his boats. Three skiffs, two canoes, a kayak, three motors (thirty, forty, and fifty horse), dozens of life preservers, towels, insulated picnic baskets and those oars. Mr. Dana was prepared to take a party of twenty out to the mid-Atlantic for a picnic. But gasoline was too expensive. It was on principle that he never left the boathouse. And he was too fat to fit in his kayak.

You'd think him benign, almost babyish. There was

nothing loud, threatening or even alert about him. He always seemed to be just waking up. The remaining wisps of baby fine hair disheveled, sleepy half-closed eyes, wrinkled clothes. And yet he ran his boathouse like a navy officer. Everything had its place. Boats were freshly painted, green to the water line, white above, buoys to match. He would miss that oar tomorrow morning. And when I returned it, he'd give me hell. After all, how many opportunities would he get to lay out an oar thief? I entertained thoughts of never bringing it back, of turning professional.

I took the oar and hoped he wouldn't catch me before I reached the boat. The skiff was a short ways off if I walked along the rocks. The forest spooked me, and would now be much less lit than the rocks. The moon was hidden behind the clouds, but its dim, filtered light was better than nothing.

The oarlock didn't quite fit but I hammered it halfway into the slot with a rock. I pushed off and began rowing against the current.

It was almost over. I had to work twice as hard because the current was against me. The boat was still in one piece. Except for a few stubs and scratches my feet weren't badly hurt. I was considering that I'd never be hired as a foot model when a high wave slammed against the side of the boat. It knocked me off my seat into six inches of water that had leaked in. This damn boat would never seize up. Far as I was concerned it was going back to the shop tomorrow morning. I could afford to think about tomorrow morning since I was close by the floating Christian—my haul off. More on the right. Hold up on the left. I had never been so happy to see a cross, let alone a floating one, in all my childhood years attending St. George's Episcopal. I grabbed hold of the buoy, first time, and tied it onto the boat. I was home. I was safe. I grabbed the haul off and pulled myself into shore.

A hot bath, a hot meal, a little booze, a warm bed. I could allow myself to feel cold and uncomfortable now. Before, it would have been too dangerous a luxury.

The water was momentarily still. The ocean seemed to respect me and rewarded me by rolling out a carpet of calmness. I stepped off the boat like a royal admiral whose ceremonial landing is never marred by mishaps.

Why I Wrote 'The Sailboat'

"Writing is like baking a cake": one of my mother's adages. Everything is like baking a cake: a pinch of this, a taste of that, and don't forget the raisins. Or the chocolate chips, or whatever else is your favorite additive: humor, whimsy, lyrical or descriptive passages, experiments with form: three paragraphs here, a sentence there, a sentence here.

You yourself ought to try one of the assignments you give your students. There's nothing like experience. The reason you value writing so much, the reason you're bothering to read this book, is because you probably like to write. So why aren't you doing it?

The act of writing can be intimidating and lonely. It forces you into yourself, brings you close to your feelings about yourself and what you produce. It's good enough; it's not good enough.

Why did I write "The Sailboat"? To tell the truth, just to share it with you. In the same way, you should share your work with your students. As you read their writing, let them read yours—as much as is comfortable for you and them. If not a whole story, at least a part. In sharing, a part is as good as a whole. The important thing is the *sharing*. Through it comes an acceptance of your own work. As soon as self-consciousness rubs off, reading one another's work becomes just one more daily or common class experience: ho-hum stuff not so fraught with the anxiety "Am I good enough?"

Try to write along with your class. Don't spend that quiet time checking all your roll books, making remarks for the record files, or doing any of the put-off paper work that teachers are bombarded with and rarely have time for. If you write along with your students and share your writing with them, a book like this one will begin to work exactly as it ought to, as a springboard for your *own* invention.

You are a creative teacher. You've probably proved it in a zillion ways. So now just relax and try to enjoy writing as much as you'd like your students to enjoy it.

Pretend you're doing it for them!

Recipes for Adventure

You are climbing a hill. You must get to the top! There is something you must do there. (Rescue someone, bring water or food to a starving group, deliver a letter, etc.) Time is running out. The hill is so hard to climb. The terrain itself is your enemy. It fights you every inch of the way. (It may be a sand dune, with the sand crumbling underneath your feet, or it may be a jagged cliff that you are climbing without shoes. It may be a snow-covered mountain, icy and slippery.) Do you make it to the top or do you slip or fall? Describe your ascent or descent in detail. What do you see? What helps or hinders you in your climb?

You start out on a routine trip. (Perhaps to the grocery or to visit a relative, or you may be on the subway going to your dentist.) But suddenly something unexpected happens, and your course must change completely. How do you adapt to the new condition? Where do you wind up?

You are trapped in an old abandoned building, in a

desolate part of town. (How did you get there and why?) Night is approaching, and the streets are empty. You bang on the windows and shout, but no one is around to hear you. To make matters worse, you were supposed to deliver a very important message, but it now looks as if you'll never complete the assignment. (It could be a matter of life and death.) What goes through your mind? Are you frightened? By what? Describe the house, the rooms and furniture, as twilight grows into nighttime. Are there rats? Weird noises? Do you escape? How?

You are a stranger in a city you do not know. You are walking alone at night. You are a strong person, but you are lonely. You have come to this city for a reason. (Why?) The people you pass on the street remind you of the secret job you have come to do. Try to match the mood of the city with your own.

You have been caught! Knocked unconscious by your enemies, you wake up in a dark cell with no windows. There is no way out: you cannot even find a door. You wonder where you are. Start recalling all the events that led to your capture. (Tell the story as it happens or as a flashback.)

You awaken to find yourself in a room you do not recognize. Everything is strange and unfamiliar. You begin to explore. You find something, a note, a letter, a newspaper article, that makes you realize you have been kidnaped. Why? Where are you? Who are the kidnapers? Describe your room and the sensation of strangeness and unfamiliarity. Are you in danger? How do you feel?

Your kidnapers have mistaken you for someone else. You try to explain this to them, but they do not believe you. How can you convince them that you are not the person they think you are? (A birthmark? A photo? Forthrightness and sincerity?)

You *must* get something that is locked away in a high security vault. In order to reach the vault, you must travel through a very narrow tunnel, hardly wide enough for your body. You slither on your belly. You must not touch the top of the tunnel, which is only inches away from your body. If you do, a loud alarm will go off and water will gush into the tunnel and drown you. As you slither along toward the vault you are talking to yourself. (What are you saying?) What is in the vault? (A valuable document? Jewels? Money?) Are you on the side of the law or are you a thief? A spy? Do you make it to the vault? How do you get inside? (Dynamite? You know the numbers on the combination lock?) Do you succeed or fail in your mission?

You wake up one day and find that you are no longer a human being. You may be a mouse, a butterfly, a small bird or insect. What happens to you? Variation: You wake up one morning and find that you are blind. You are also amnesiac. Your sight slowly returns, but your memory doesn't. You meet people who know you but whom you do not recognize. You begin living a life not really your own. Describe your daily routine, and your feelings at going through the motions without knowing who you are. Do you ever discover your identity? How did you become amnesiac?

As a baby you were abandoned in a large forest or jungle. There you were adopted by animals (wolves or monkeys or elephants, etc.) who brought you up to be like themselves. Describe how you came to the forest, your first impressions of that dark greenness. Describe what growing up was like for you. Who are your friends, your enemies? What did you learn, and how? How do you live? Eat? Sleep?

You have been away from home and family for many years. (Why? Where were you? What were you doing there?) Now you are returning home. But on the way you meet someone. (Who? Where?) This person does not want you to reach home (why?), so he gives you the wrong directions. You are led off course and end up going somewhere else entirely, perhaps a dangerous or exciting place. You may end up on a ship leaving for a foreign port; or on a deserted dead-end street, where someone lies waiting for you; or in a burlap bag being transported to who knows where.

You are trying to find a person, place or thing that is very important to you. (What is it, and why is it important?) Describe your experiences and adventures during the search. There may be people who don't want you to reach your goal, and they may do things to stop you. Storms may slow you up or make you take cover for a while. You may also run into rivals. Do you reach your goal or do you fail?

You have been away for a very long time, and now you want to go back home. You start out, but before you reach your destination you are captured by someone, who may or may not have magical powers (depending on the kind of story you want to tell), and who says that before he will let you go you must pass several tests of strength and endurance. The tests may be torturous: you may have to swim in mud, or be tickled for an hour without laughing. Describe the tests. How do you perform? Does your captor let you go? Do you escape? Do you turn the tables on your captor?

You have been searching for her for years, nearly all your life. Why? You think you have finally found her. She is behind that door; all you have to do is open it. (Where is the door?) You open it, but you can't believe what you see!

You have been searching for this special place for years and years. Finally you find it. Why is the place so special? Does it live up to your expectations? How do you feel? (The place may be a natural setting, a home, a house, a magic cave, or an entrance into the earth where treasure is hidden, etc. There are thousands of possibilities.)

Have you ever been caught without shelter in a really bad rainstorm? How did it feel to be soaked to the skin? To be out of the storm, and safe, warm and dry?

Describe the worst rainstorm, snowstorm, hailstorm or thunderstorm you ever saw. Where were you when it happened? What thoughts ran through your mind?

The Researched Adventure

Is it possible to write an adventure story without having lived it? Of course, as many an adventure novelist will assure you. An author needs to know enough about her adventure, however, to convince her reader to come aboard her sailboat or roll along on her covered wagon. A little research on means of transportation or ways of life can inspire an adventure story, especially if the teacher asks the right questions and provides creative support.

To begin a researched adventure, you might draw up, with the help of your students, a list of activities in which they are interested. The list can include activities they have actually undertaken and those they would like to undertake one day. Let each of the students choose one activity from the list, research it, then, create an adventure around it. The research is less important than the idea that the student will *know* something about her subject matter. Even if she doesn't include new-found information, she still will have acquired the experience of writing an adventure story inspired by reality.

If your student gets stuck and doesn't know what to do next, you might advise her to put her hero in a different situation and then get him out of it. How? By using whatever she knows on her own or has learned through her research. In fiction, anything is possible.

Your student has experienced enough to write about certain feelings. Just because she has never held onto a rope a few feet from the bottom of a dark and deep well, this does not mean that she cannot describe the experience. She has known fear, waiting, hope, the dark, water, exhaustion. She has probably even experienced holding onto a rope. If she hasn't, bring some rope into class, tie it up and let her hold onto it for a long time, with her eyes closed perhaps, in the back of the class: then have her write down her impressions of this experience or use it in her story.

Recipes

The teacher can prepare a list of natural disasters: floods, landslides, volcanic eruptions, hurricanes. Ask students to research one, then describe it as it is taking place, putting themselves in or near it. Do they escape? How do they protect themselves? How does it feel to be near something so violent as it is happening?

You are on your way someplace, but the weather makes it impossible for you to go on. Where are you? Do you make it to a hotel? A cave or other shelter? The cold, heat, rain, fog or snow grows worse. How do you stay alive? How do you keep comfortable, safe, how do you sleep, eat, keep from going crazy?

You are driving home and a great snowstorm begins to rage. You are worried. Everything around you is white and confusing. You can barely see where you are going. Suddenly your car stalls. You are far from home and don't really know where you are. Now you can't see a thing. What do you do? Do you stay in your car or leave it? How do you keep alive and warm? (You may even have a special reason for wanting to get home, which makes the situation more dramatic. You may need to bring someone medicine or an important message or letter.)

A hurricane blows your house away. (What is it like to see things around you ripped or sucked away?) What are your feelings? Where do you go? Where are you hiding as you watch this? How do you protect yourself, if you are not hiding? How do you survive: eat, sleep, stay warm, etc.?

A tornado springs up without warning. You are playing in your tree house. You cling to the tree. What happens to you? What is going on around you?

A flood has turned your neighborhood into a river. You are floating on a boat or raft, and you can see all the housetops sticking out of the water. What is this sensation like? What other things float past you? Are you trying to row or float some place in particular, or do you just free-float? What happens? You see your neighbors float past you. What kinds of things do you say to one another?

Research the Bermuda Triangle, then write as though you were on a ship going through it. What happens to you?

You are exploring an unknown territory. Part of your mission is to draw a map of the area, including the road you took, and any special geographic points of interest, including ponds, brooks, poison-ivy patches, man-eating plants, trout streams, blueberry bushes, bear caves, etc. You want your map to be of use to others who will traverse this area. Draw this map. After having drawn it, describe the journey you took, stage by stage; include descriptions of all the things you passed. If there are people living in this territory, describe their habits and eccentricities. Are they friendly or warlike? If they are warlike, instruct future travelers how to get along with them. (Should they offer them food? Candy? Cigarettes? Kiss them? Ignore them? Sneeze twice and turn around? Imitate the ceremonial greeting of crossing your eyes and jumping up and down three times, and flapping the arms?) Remember, you want to help future travelers, by describing as accurately as possible what they can expect to find in the territory. You are also suggesting the best routes or paths to take: "Fourteen feet from the big rock to the small trout stream. Turn left and walk half a mile to the big dead tree with mushrooms growing on it. There you will find a patch of berries. Do not eat them."

Your plane has crashed in the jungle. You have only a few days' supply of water and food. How do you survive?

The teacher can take her students on an outing to the park or countryside. Ask them to look at a large hill or mountain and then to compose a letter or speech to the mountain. Try to have them think of themselves as mountain climbers before the ascent: they are talking to the mountain, complimenting it, teasing it, challenging it, warning it (i.e. "I'll get to the top of you, you little ant hill, you'll see").

Variation of the above: the teacher asks her students to imagine themselves climbing the mountain and to describe the climb in realistic detail. Or, better yet, let them climb the mountain and record their progress, changes in flora, the sensation of getting warm or out of breath, fatigue, etc. Let them write as they walk, stopping every time they experience something to jot it down. The writing is, in effect, a diary or record of a physical event. The focus should be on changes in their own body sensations and in external particulars during their walk.

You are a quarter of an inch big. You dive into an aquarium. What happens? Are there people looking into the aquarium? Do they see you?

As a deep-sea diver, you are given an assignment that takes you to the very bottom of the ocean. What is the ocean floor like? How dark is the ocean? Is the water roiled or still? What color is the ocean? What assignment are you on? You may run into danger. (A large fish, a man-eating plant, an octopus, getting caught in an old rusty ship or locked in a cabin. The class might prepare a list of the kinds of possible adventures or dangers at the bottom of the ocean.)

Research an animal and its behavior. One animal might be a wolf. Try to imagine life in a wolf pack or animal society. Describe it from the point of view of a wolf. In every animal society there are leaders and followers, and some animals have special jobs, like guarding and watching over the babies, or finding food and bringing it back to the pack or group. You might write as a wolf, or any other animal you choose, with a special job in the pack. Describe everyday life. Imagine that something unusual happens to interrupt this daily routine. (A hunter, a rainstorm, getting caught in a trap, fighting with a larger animal.)

You are an animal who is taken from your rightful home (natural home like the woods, or a domestic home with a master). Who steals you and why? Do you try to get back to your original home or do you decide to stay with your kidnaper? Why?

You are a cowboy. You ride into a strange town, expecting to stay just long enough to get a good night's rest. Unfortunately, you get into a fight with a mean desperado. The morning after the fight the desperado returns to town, just as you are leaving, with a gang of fifteen outlaws. You are outnumbered, but you manage to defeat them all. Describe how you do it.

Compile a list of the most exciting things to do or experience that you can think of. These will include things you've done as well as things you've never done. (The teacher may run this particular activity for a week or longer, or for one lesson only. The advantage of a longer time period is that it gives the students a chance to think up many more possibilities. The possibilities are of course all story ideas.)

What does "exciting" mean?

What does "danger" mean? What are dangerous things? Were you ever in danger?

Ask both of your parents to tell you (or best of all, write with you) the most exciting experience they ever had, or the most dangerous situation they were ever in.

Does something have to be dangerous to be exciting?

Where is the most exciting place on earth? Why? How would you get there? What would you do once you were there?

You are in a contest of strength with a dangerous rival. (You may be thumb-wrestling, boxing, fencing, dueling.) Describe the physical movements made by the two of you while attacking and defending. Where are you? (In a house, room, open field.) How do your surroundings help or hurt your position? What is going through your mind as you attack? As you defend?

Who is the toughest person you know? Describe him or her so that we see and experience the person as you do.

How does a tough person get to be so tough?

You are brave, courageous. Tell a weaker person or a coward how to be brave, courageous, fearless and strong.

Write a monologue of a weak and frightened person who has just been humiliated (perhaps through name calling or physical force) but who cannot stand up for his or her rights and is always being pushed around.

You have been on a long, difficult journey. You had many adventures and experiences. Now you are returning home. (How? Walking? By boat? Train?) Describe your memories, thoughts and feelings. You may be reminiscing about your adventures and the places you've been. Are you happy or sad to be returning home? You may be thinking of people and places at home. Did you miss them or were you glad to be away from them for a while?

You are a hero, receiving a hero's homecoming. A parade and party are being held in your honor. Describe your homecoming. How do you feel about all this attention? What do people say to you? How do they look at you? What do your parents say? Do you deserve all this attention? What did you do to make you a hero? Are you a real hero or are you fooling people? (This may be written from the third person if a student wishes.)

This is the hardest, most difficult thing you've ever had to do in your life. You have just been awarded an important medal, but you know that you really do not deserve it. You are standing in front of a large audience, many of them old friends who love you. You are supposed to give an acceptance speech, but instead of accepting the medal, you decide to confess that another person deserves it. You are probably embarrassed. Write a speech in which you explain to the audience why you cannot accept the medal. Begin the speech by addressing the audience: "Ladies and Gentlemen."

Variation: Write the monologue of the person who *really* deserves the medal as he watches it being presented to another person. Try to express all the disappointment and bitterness this person would be feeling.

You led a very exciting life. (What did you do?) Now you have retired. You are thinking back to the good old days. Express your pleasure and excitement in past experiences and your boredom with your present easy way of life, which does not afford any excitement. (You may not feel bored at all, you may feel relieved.)

You fall deep into a well, but manage to grab hold of a rope. You look up and the top seems very far away, just a little circle of light above you. In your pocket you find things that help you in your try to escape: string, knife, wooden stick, deflated balloon, potato chips. (Choose two from this list or another list prepared by the teacher and classmates.) How do you use these two things to escape? How does it feel and look inside the well? How does it sound? Do you get out? How did you fall in in the first place; why were you at or near the well?

You are lost in a forest. You find two of the following things in your pocket: lighter, knife, string or rope, canteen, compass, sandwich. How do you use them to help find a way out of the forest, or to survive till help comes? What is it like to be in the forest all by yourself? Why did you go there in the first place?

You are in a desert with only two things to help you survive and find your way back to civilization. What two things would you pick and why?

You are the leader of a gang. Describe the other members of the gang. Is your gang notorious? Well liked? What do other people—neighbors, teachers, parents—think of your gang? What is the name of the gang? How did it earn that name? What are particular gang members known for? (What can they do best?) How did the gang start? If you have a real gang, or a bunch of friends, you can tell about them. What adventures have earned the gang its reputation?

You are pursuing someone, or being pursued, in a specific setting. (A warehouse, castle, cellar, school, empty movie theater, grocery or super market, bathroom, school kitchen, anywhere.) Describe how you use the place and all its resources and peculiarities to your own advantage. (For example, hiding behind boxes in a supermarket, and wheeling a shopping cart into your enemy to keep him from capturing you.)

You are being tortured. (How?) They want information from you. (Why?) Who are "they"? What do you do?

You are tied to a chair. Someone comes toward you holding a knife in his hand. Is he going to untie you or is he going to stab you?

You are following someone in a fun house. You catch up with this person in a room full of mirrors. You see her all around you because she is reflected in the mirrors, but you cannot tell which image is the real person. What goes through your mind?

An enemy has just drugged your drink. You begin to realize what's happening to you, but you're getting too drowsy to do anything about it. Describe the sensation of falling asleep while fighting to stay awake. What does it feel like finally to succumb to the drug? Where do you wake up? Who or what is the first thing you see?

You are chasing a car in your neighborhood or it is chasing

you. Describe the streets and things and people you pass, knock down, avoid hitting, etc. Describe how you escape or catch up with the car you're chasing. Try to imagine and see it happening in your neighborhood, try to see the streets, the people, the stores you know so well.

Variation: You are chasing, or being chased, in your neighborhood. You and your enemy are both on foot. Describe the way you would use your neighborhood (or school, or park) to hide from or overtake him. You might even walk around your neighborhood before you begin the story (good for class project) and make a note of a few places that seem good for hiding. You may include the street name or house number in your description so that when the piece is read aloud others in the class can locate it and get a clearer picture of what you are describing.

You are being chased by a gang, who finally corner you. You can't escape. What happens? (Where do they corner you? Why are they after you?)

You are rowing a small boat out to a large ship in the ocean. It is nighttime, very late. A war is going on. You are trying to get to the ship because you are a soldier who has just completed a mission on an island. You have destroyed an enemy munitions store. Suddenly a light shines on you. An enemy ship has spotted you! It begins to fire. You jump off the rowboat and start swimming to the ship. The shots light up the ocean all around you. Write your version of this story. You may choose to end it or not, as you wish.

You are walking on a beach. Suddenly you see something sticking out of the sand. You bend down. It is a mine! If you had stepped on it you would have been blown up! You realize that the beach is full of mines. Nevertheless, you must walk across it. (Why?) How do you walk? What are your thoughts?

Write a story entitled "Escape"; "Rescue"; "Trouble at Moosehead Lake"; "Back from Hell!"; "Survival."

Secrets: Why We Read Mysteries

Secrets. We love having them, someone else's or our own. When a friend confides in us we are gratified by such trust. Being the only one who knows makes us feel special and privileged. We keep our own secrets too because there are always things we don't want other people to know about us. For personal reasons we avoid exposing certain relationships, acts, our origins or backgrounds, sometimes our beliefs and opinions. We like to feel that we can control what people know about us and therefore what they think of us.

But secrets are not always successfully hidden. Mystery stories involve one person trying to uncover another's secret.

A crime is committed and then discovered. This is the usual starting point of all stories in the genre. But where is the secret? What is the mystery? The crime is no secret, it has already been found. The mystery (and with it the secret) lies in the criminal and her motive. And so in this genre, the story is about *who did it and why*. Because of its concern with motive, the mystery is the most fundamentally psychological

94

of all the four popular genres, and therefore perhaps the most relevant literary form we have today. Given to analyzing our own behavior, we have come to accept motive as an important part of everyday life: there are reasons behind our actions, and to analyze them correctly is to understand them . . . and ourselves.

But mysteries fascinated us long before Freud was born. Let's face it, we enjoy curiosity. It makes us feel more alive, more awake. Puzzles tickle us. We love to try to solve problems, our own, our friends', our family's, our nation's.

Our involvement in a mystery story depends largely on our interest in the character who is solving the mystery. Along the way we may turn hardboiled like Philip Marlowe, or romp in the land of harmless intrigue with the supernormal Nancy Drew and her counterparts, the Hardy Boys.

Crime solvers are quirky, eccentric, always individualistic. We love them for being down and out, or glitteringly rich and snobbish, even if we hate the same types in all other genres. Nick Charles (of *The Thin Man*) was a socialite-alcoholic, Harriet Vane was a precursor of the women's rights movement, and Nero Wolfe loved to eat. But all have the ability to ferret out discordant facts and observations and deduce from them the truth *as it really happened*.

Mystery solvers feel the illegality of situations with a kind of sixth sense unique to them. They are the most observant of all genre heroes. Like the prototypal detective Sherlock Holmes, they must have a feel for warm teacups and an eye for crumbs and stray hairs. They notice the misplaced vase, the muddy shoeprint on the carpet and the initialed matchbox left behind on the dresser, and from these clues they reconstruct the truth. They meditate on the illogical or puzzling aspects of each mystery, treating them like the pieces of a largr jigsaw puzzle. They are as curious as they are idealistic in their search for the truth.

At some point, the mystery solver is usually called upon to risk his life. For the mystery is a story of survival—survival by one's wits. The detective always noses around too much for his own good. It is his strength as well as his curse. What saves him is his clever mind, his intuition and his ability to make sense out of all the seemingly unimportant details that he has noticed and absorbed. His judgment of suspects and what to expect from them is so shrewd that he may safely take physical risks, which in turn lead him to the capture of the criminal and the solution of the crime.

People of all ages like to think that they can outsmart other people. Understanding a character's motives and foretelling his actions are proof of getting older and smarter. Children especially like to say, "I told you so," and "I knew he would do that."

Students who write and read in this genre are testing their reasoning power. They like to put two and two together. Craftiness and the ability to ferret out information, to draw conclusions, to control dramatic situations, to make critical decisions and to take physical risks: having to render all these qualities cannot help but challenge your students' imaginations.

You may be afraid that students will not be able to write a mystery because of its complexities and its interwoven elements. Yet precisely these features make it so valuable to them. The mystery genre demands control over one's material. It isn't that a writer must have her story set in her mind perfectly before she tells it, but that she must learn *how* to tell it. A mystery unfolds more calculatedly than any other type of story because it must maintain suspense. The writer creates suspense for her readers by controlling the amount and type of information given to them or kept from them.

Students are rarely expected to control their material, yet it is possible for them to learn to do so while writing mysteries. I've found the dictation process particularly helpful to some of my students. While writing a complete mystery, they may get frustrated by the necessity for having to hold a lot of information in their heads. I help my students by sharing the physical task of writing with them: some of the time, they dictate and I write. I also try to bring to light discrepancies where they exist, so that the mystery stays fairly logical.

The mystery story lends itself well to the building-up method. It is a genre whose elements are plain to see: criminal, suspects, witnesses, clues, detective. Each of these elements could make a story by itself; together they make a mystery.

The mystery may seem too complicated to write, but it is within the grasp of your students: it is a sophisticated form of story telling, but so much can be learned from it that it is well worth trying.

Elements of a Mystery

First things first. There must be a crime, or at least a crime-in-the-making. The crime may be against a person: a murder, a rape, a mugging, a hold-up, blackmail, or a kidnaping. Or it may be against an object, usually one that has special value or meaning to its owner: a jewel, a vase, a manuscript, a good-luck charm, a car with important documents hidden in its glove compartment. A crime may also be committed against a place: a church or park vandalized; a tennis club destroyed; a house bombed; a patch of land or beach booby-trapped.

The crime, or crime-in-the-making, must be discovered. Without discovery there would be no mystery story. Who discovers the crime, and how does the discovery take place? The discoverer may be an innocent bystander who later becomes the prime suspect, a relative, a maid, the narrator, a detective, the police, a child. Any one of them may force open a locked door and find a body crumpled up nearby, routinely open a safe to find a diamond tiara gone, take a dip in a pool and encounter a corpse fully dressed at the bottom with rocks in his pockets.

After the crime has been discovered, the mystery solver steps onto the scene. He may be a police officer, detective, private citizen, curious neighbor or relative. His motive for taking on the case may be personal interest, love, familial responsibility, curiosity, money or sentiment.

The mystery solver first tries to ascertain whether anyone has seen anything that might be relevant to the case. Enter the witnesses. Witnesses are accidental or purposeful observers who have seen a crime or a very suspicious occurrence. Very rarely does a witness see the crime as it happened. More often she sees or hears part of it: sees a leg as the criminal runs out the door, hears a loud noise and happens to look at her watch. Witnesses observe with varying degrees of accuracy. What they think they have seen they may not have. A witness may not tell the truth because she is protecting herself or someone else. Or she may simply have seen or heard in a faulty or partial manner.

Next come the suspects, those seemingly guilty characters any one of whom had motive and opportunity enough to commit the crime. Some suspects seem more obviously guilty than others, but there is no way of identifying the real culprit from outward appearances alone. A character becomes a suspect because she is found near or at the scene of the crime, or because she has no alibi at the time the crime was committed. But, most important, she must have a motive. Motive and suspect are inextricably intwined.

As I said earlier, the mystery story is much more psychological in nature than the other genres because of its concern with motive. Motive is in a sense nothing less than a case history, a study in human behavior. A character's motives stem from her "secret self," that part of the personality which readers and viewers of the mystery love to see exposed. It is never enough to know how a crime was done and by whom; we want to know why it was done. Some writers attempt to give the motive behind the motive: X killed his father because X hated his father. Why did X hate his father? Because he was cut out of his father's will. Why? Because X had married against the old man's wishes. Why? X was rebelling against the old man. Motives may include revenge, jealousy, lust, greed, altruism, fear of blackmail, fear of exposure of one's past, abnormality.

The criminal in a mystery story never succeeds entirely in covering up his tracks. The detective finds clues that implicate, or lead him to, the criminal. Clues may be objects that belong to the criminal or that are in some way associated with him. A lighter left behind at the scene of the crime may bear his initials, for example. The murder weapon itself may provide a clue, as may a set of fingerprints, a piece of clothing, a comb, a handkerchief, a heel off a shoe. Some clues may be in the form of information or statements provided by suspects, witnesses or other characters.

The mystery solver follows suspects and is himself often followed. Almost always a chase of some sort takes place that moves the story to a high pitch of excitement and adventure. In some novels, the chase lasts all book long. A chase is usually physical but may also have aspects of a contest in which criminal and mystery solver try to outwit each other.

The mystery ends with a confession, which the criminal may make voluntarily or at the point of a gun. Through it the true story emerges and loose ends are cleared up.

The mystery is commonly thought of as sensational, but it does not necessarily have to make the hair stand on end. Its prime satisfaction is intellectual: the reader takes part in the mystery solver's mental gymnastics and may even compete with him by trying to reach a solution before he does.

The Missing Coat:
A Mystery Game for the Classroom

The teacher had just finished the writing lesson. She was a pretty good teacher. At least she liked to think she was. She had gerbils, turtles and rabbits in her class. She let students take turns eating lunch in the room with her. She held group discussions about feelings in the quiet corner. She had airplane model projects, complex sewing and cooking projects. She had trained young student teachers who had liked her and learned from her. How could she doubt she was a good teacher? She *was* a good teacher. But today she was going to try something she'd never tried before. Would she hurt them? Would they think she was crazy? Would she do it so badly that they'd never trust her again?

The class was to have recess in the yard today. It was spring and the children were beginning to go haywire. They were all scrambling for their coats, jostling one another on the way to the coat closet. The teacher's feelings were slightly hurt. It had been a good writing lesson. Why did they always prefer basketball to writing stories? They had zipped through the lesson easily, eager to get it over with sooner and have more time for play. If only she could have made her lesson more like play.

Children were buttoning up jackets, tying already discarded sweaters around their waists. "Class!" The lineup was beginning by the front door. The teacher checked her watch, fingered the whistle hanging from her neck lanyard. "Stop what you're doing, Laurie, and get in line." Laurie was so meek and submissive, always being ordered around by her best friend, Becky; it was unusual for her not to follow the teacher's orders immediately. It might have occurred to the teacher that something was wrong, but if she had this feeling she chose, for some reason, to disregard it. She turned off the lights and the class began filing out. Then she felt pulls at her sweater. It was Laurie.

"I can't find my jacket," she whined.

The teacher felt a twinge of irresponsibility. Hurting a child, was that what she was doing? She had never felt so doubtful about herself as a teacher, yet so excited.

"I looked everywhere."

The teacher turned the lights on and sat down at her desk. She was going to go through with it no matter what. It was a good idea, she knew it was. "Everyone!" she commanded, "look for Laurie's jacket right *now*. Look in desks, cubbyholes, the closet, look all over. There will be no recess until it's found."

No basketball—what a disappointment! A groan went up. Reluctantly they asked questions.

"What does it look like?"

"Where did you put it?"

"Are you sure you took it today?"

"Yes, I took it. And it's green leather."

"What *color* green, Laurie?" Sarah was exasperated.

"Dark. It has pearl buttons and a belt at the back."

They weren't catching on. Well. Part of her wanted them to see through it right away. Then she wouldn't have to go through with it. She didn't dare get cold feet now.

The class looked but found nothing. José and Michael began to joke around. They exchanged mock punches.

"Hey, man, where'd you *put* that jacket anyway?"

"I didn't take it," said José, annoyed but laughing. "You mother ___."

Michael had José in a fake headlock. José elbowed Michael. "You mother ___, let me go!" Both were enjoying the play.

"Michael and José, stop that immediately! Now help look for that jacket!"

"We been lookin', we been lookin'," Michael bopped.

"Yeah, where'd she hide it anyway?"

The children within earshot of this remark found it uproarious, and even the teacher smiled. At least they were enjoying it. All those times she'd wanted to strangle Michael. She was only too glad to have him now. She'd have to encourage this more during the next hour. At least, let it happen and not squash it.

The search had yielded nothing. The children were fidgeting. A water fight was brewing at the sink.

"We can't find it. Can we go out now?"

"No. You'll have to try harder."

"We already *looked* everywhere." They were losing patience with her. Take the reins, be the authority, crack the whip. It's the only way.

"You haven't asked enough of the right questions." They didn't really understand what she was talking about. They'd think that she was crazy. She was sinking. Her only chance was to sound like she knew what she was talking about.

"You've been reading mysteries, haven't you? Well, here's a chance to use what you know. What kind of questions do detectives ask in mystery stories?"

"Did anyone see it get stolen?" "When did Laurie last see the jacket?" "Did she have a fight with anyone?" "Did she have enemies who might have stolen her jacket?"

To some degree, the teacher thought, they were asking these questions just to please her. This was the beauty part of teaching. When all the hard work to get them to trust you paid off. They were willing to go along just because she had asked them to. They didn't consider whether they would get anything out of this. They were doing her a favor because they liked her.

"I had an argument with Nina," Laurie said, "but I don't think *she* stole my jacket."

Nina struck an indignant pose and spoke with a snooty British accent. "I cer-tain-ly did *not*." Nina was well developed and much more mature than the rest of them, yet she too went along and played. Everyone seemed good-natured and cooperative.

"Wait!" Sherrae had a brainstorm. But instead of saying it aloud, she uncharacteristically whispered it to Donna, who announced, "Maybe someone in Ms. Brayboy's class saw the jacket. We lined up with them this morning. Could we go there and find out?"

"I don't want to go," Sherrae said, glancing at the teacher, who shrugged and said, "All right, Donna, just you go." Sherrae was always loud and outspoken, never coy. Why was she acting so unlike herself?

Then James said in his ponderously thoughtful way, "Maybe we should ask in Mr. Breindel's class." So James and Freddie and Jésus left the classroom in search of someone who might know something about the missing jacket.

Charles said that a lot of times stolen things ended up in the bathrooms. Maybe he should check those.

Tracey disagreed. The jacket was more likely to have been stuffed in a garbage can.

"Maybe someone should ask the maintenance man."

"Or look in the yard."

"No! The stairways."

"The lunchroom!"

Not only had they taken the bait, they had started a game

within a game. They had devised ways to leave the classroom!

Before long the teacher found herself in an empty room. This was it. The end. Even a principal like Mr. Mercado would find it hard to understand a classroom with no children in it at 11 o'clock in the morning. And they had all gone with her blessing. She had given everyone, including Laurie, fifteen minutes to conduct their searches. Only Sherrae stayed behind to give the room a final once-over. She looked behind curtains and bookshelves and through the coat closet again. Then she asked to see the teacher's coat closet, but the teacher said she had already looked in there herself.

The others returned running, out of breath, noisy, misbehaving, impossible to quiet down, and without information or clues to offer. Exhilarated by their searches, they had entered in the spirit of the mystery. In their enthusiasm they were inviting her to carry them further into it.

"Did anyone see anything this morning, anything at all that might in some small way help us to solve this?"

"I saw Laurie take the jacket and hang it up. But that's all I saw, I swear." Good old paranoid, show-off Becky, acting true to form in her desire to be cast in this drama as Laurie's best friend, which she was, and to bolster her image as perpetually honest and innocent.

"We know you didn't do it, Becky."

"Me? Oh my God! I'm as honest a creature as ever *you'll* run across!" she sniggered. "I give dimes back to supermarket clerks. *Supermarket* clerks!"

"Maybe," Gene shouted, "maybe it fell to the floor and someone who came into the class dragged it outside." The image of someone sliding the jacket along the floor was outlandish. She didn't want this getting silly, but she did pursue the idea of outsiders.

The class recollected the various monitors who had entered the room. But Sarah, James and the teacher were certain that they had not left the front of the room during the monitors' visit.

105

That left the possibility of an inside job.

"What about the class. Do you think we have any suspects in here?" The class broke out laughing. It was coming. The surprise. The celebration. The payoff. The birthday cake. She *knew* her class. She felt like kicking her heels. They had not been outraged at her question. They had been energized by conducting their own search and interrogation. They had left the room with self-imposed assignments: places to search, people to question. They had invented and pursued their own theories, some of them bizarre. (A jacket hidden behind the coke machine in the second floor teachers' lounge?)

"You did it, you culprit." Michael had James in a headlock now, but James, so much bigger than Michael, forced his way out of the hold like a tolerant old bear.

"It was Michael," one girl teased, anticlimactically, desperately wanting him to like her. But Michael was oblivious to all but the attention he was now getting.

"I didn't do it!" He spun his bent body exaggeratedly on his heels, pointed an imaginary gun and said with a dopey leer, "It must've been José."

José did not like being accused even in jest. He protested angrily, "I didn't take no goddamn jacket, shithead!" But it was hard to maintain a straight face with Michael standing frozen in his ridiculous pose. That was Michael. He would persist even in a corny joke until he got some response.

"All right. Let's get serious for a while." The teacher passed out pieces of paper. "If you have a suspect, write the name down. But there's one rule. You can't write a name down unless you can supply a motive. No suspect without a motive."

While her students were writing, the teacher looked at her wrist watch. The preliminaries had taken more than an hour. The class was feeling good. She was feeling good. Now if only it ended as well as it had begun!

Very few papers were passed to the front of the room. The suspects naturally included Michael, James and José, also the

106

school bully, and herself. How should she handle this? Could she pull it off successfully?

"Hey! How did *my* name get on the list of suspects?" Let it run its natural course; don't blow it. Show concern, serious adult concern. Just a touch of shocked authority. "Who wrote that?"

Sherrae raised her hand and smiled discreetly.

"Why do you think it's *me*, Sherrae?" The teacher looked surprised.

"Well, when I was in the room with you looking around and I asked you if I could look in your closet, you looked . . . you looked funny."

The teacher had not been aware of any change of expression. She wanted to deny it. She thought she had hardly blinked an eye. She felt a tinge of annoyance; really the child was being too critical. But no. She was caught. She was caught, and this was how it felt to be caught. She had to suppress a surprising instinct to fight against it.

"You had a . . . a light in your eye. Like a funny gleam. I don't know." Sherrae struggled to put it into words; "I just knew you were the one."

"And my motive?"

"I don't know." Sherrae shook her head. "Was it to give us some fun? *Was* it you?" She had surprised herself, being right.

The class had heard this dialogue but had not absorbed it. They were still, quiet, eyes squinted, heads cocked.

"Can anyone help Sherrae with why I might have taken Laurie's jacket?"

"Well," said Leslie cautiously, "you made a mystery."

"Yeah!" Sherrae stood up. "That's it. She was teaching us about mysteries today in writing. I'll never forget your face!"

"You did it?"

"It *was* you?"

"You?"

They all kept asking her, Had she done it? One slapped her

107

on the back, "Man, you had *me* fooled!"

"I never thought it was *you*." Kenny shook his head.

"I thought you was going to ask us to pay for it next!"

"How come you did that?"

"It was *writing*, you dumb idiot!" Hadn't he gotten the point yet, Yolanda wanted to know.

"Writing? That was no writing! We was finding a coat." You couldn't fool Leroy.

They all wanted to make sure they had gotten the punch line. The teacher shrugged and handed Sherrae the key to her coat closet. Inside, hanging safe and sound on a wire hanger, was Laurie's jacket.

Missing jacket, clues, witnesses, suspects, motives; the mystery had run its course. Perhaps another class might have put two and two together right away. After all, they had just had that writing lesson in which they discussed the elements of mysteries. But it had taken this class the better part of a morning; making guesses about clues, witnesses, suspects, and motives and following them up. The mystery could have been solved by logic, but it had been solved by intuition instead: one of the sleuths had observed a slight but meaningful change of expression on the face of the criminal. That sixth sense the crime solver must have, that extra feel for a mystery; she couldn't get that across in a lesson. Experience had been a better teacher.

She had turned her class into a stage, and they had performed a mystery drama. She had directed it, with help from the actors. Had they known what was going on? Had they wanted to play it out to the very end anyway? At times during the morning she had felt their eagerness to please, their almost conscious drive to enjoy the situation and make the most of it. They had almost worked at going along, coming up with those search parties! At other times she was certain that they were completely caught in the story—hood-winked. Had she truly been the director, or had they conspired to go along for the fun of it? Was it their secret or hers? She would never know. It was a mystery.

Recipes for Mystery

Make a list of possible crimes. Has anyone you know ever been the victim of a crime? What were his feelings? Your feelings when you heard about it? Have you witnessed crimes on TV? Read about them? If real crimes are so upsetting, why do most of us enjoy watching them on TV, reading detective stories or, as children, playing cops and robbers? (This is meant for discussion, but you can also turn it into a writing idea.)

You have just discovered that a crime has been committed. (What crime?) What is the first thing that comes into your mind? What do you say to yourself? What do you do? (Call the police? Run away in fear of being implicated? Cry? Scream? Freeze?)

You are found by the police at the scene of a crime you did not commit. (What was the crime? Who was the victim? Who are you? Do you know the victim?) What do you say as the police take you away? What are you thinking? How does it feel to be riding in a police car? How do the police treat you? Do they believe that you are guilty? Have you tried to explain your presence at the scene of the crime?

You enter a room (Where? What room? Specify where you are, why you are there, etc.) just in time to see an unidentified person fleeing. In the room you find indications of a crime (a dead body, an object smashed to pieces on the floor, evidence of theft, etc.). Suddenly you notice something that the criminal may have left behind. You know the owner of the object. You think you know who the criminal is! What is the object? Whom does it belong to, and how do you know? If he is the criminal, what might be his motive? Do you like this person? You may decide to turn the information over to the police, or you may take matters into your own hands by confronting him with the clue. Write a dialogue between you and him. How does he respond when you show him the evidence? Does he deny it? Does he assault you, threaten your life or run away? Or does he break down, confess and win your sympathy? What story does he tell you? (The story will of course supply a motive.) Or does he deny the accusation and claim that the object you found was really a plant left by someone trying to incriminate him?

How do you hire a good detective? How do you hear about him? How can you be sure he is honest? How much does a detective earn? Does a detective work only for money? (Good for discussion.)

What does a detective's office look like? Does the detective resemble his office? (If the office is dingy, is the detective dingy-looking too?) Read to your class some of Raymond Chandler's descriptions of Philip Marlowe's office: "The pebbled glass door panel is lettered in flaked black paint: 'Philip Marlowe . . . Investigations.' It is a reasonably shabby door at the end of a reasonably shabby corridor. . . ." "It was empty of everything but the smell of dust. I threw up another window, unlocked the communicating door and went into the room beyond. Three hard chairs and a swivel chair, flat desk with a glass top, five filing cases, three of them full of nothing, a calendar and a framed license on the wall, a phone, a washbowl in a stained wood cupboard, a hatrack, a carpet that was just something on the floor and two open windows with net curtains that puckered in and out like the lips of a toothless old man sleeping." (From *The Little Sister* and *The High Window*, both by Chandler.)

What does a detective look like? (Try to render the stereotypes.) What does the phrase "private eye" suggest? What images does it bring to mind?

Write a dialogue in which someone hires a detective. She will have to tell the detective about the case and he may mention possible suspects and motives. Does the detective accept the assignment? Does he ask questions as she tells her story? Is he suspicious? Describe the physical appearance of both characters and the detective's office. Describe the feelings of the characters, perhaps including some interior monologue. (The teacher might try reading to her class this kind of scene from a good mystery story she knows.)

You are a private eye. A person walks into your office and says, "I need your help. I'm into something over my head." You say, "Let's hear about it." She says, "It all started when . . ." What is the story she tells you? Do you take the case?

You are a private eye. A big tough approaches you on the street, twists your arm behind your back and says, "Forget about the Molloy case! We don't like the way you're nosin' around, see?" What is the Molloy case? Who sent this tough to warn you off? What does he look like? What do you say to him?

What is a shady character? What does he do to make him seem shady?

It was exactly 8:30 at night when (*name*) appeared at (*place*). She did not seem to notice the two men watching her. She walked very quickly toward the _____. "Let's go," said one of the men to the other. "She's our mystery woman." Can you explain and develop this incident in a story? Why is the woman being followed? Who are the men following her?

A crime has been committed. (What is the crime?) There are three suspects in the case. Give the name, the occupation, a physical description, a personal history, all pertinent facts (arrested once, has a child, hates dogs, blue eyes, etc.) of each suspect. Also include possible motives for committing the crime. Do the suspects know one another? Do they have anything to say about one another?

In order for a suspect to be a suspect, she must have a motive, a possible reason for having committed the crime. Imagine a crime, and a suspect or a few suspects. What was the suspect's relationship to the victim of the crime? (Was she the victim's sister, cousin, mother? Was she in love with the victim? Was she being blackmailed by the victim?) What might have been her motive?

Sometimes the way a suspect walks, talks or acts makes her appear suspicious. Pick a partner who will act as a suspect and follow her around the school or neighborhood. She will try to act suspicious while you record suspicious things she does. Describe at least ten suspicious mannerisms, acts, gestures, occurrences, etc. After half an hour or so you might switch roles, and she will follow you around as you act suspiciously.

You are a witness. Tell what you have seen. Remember, you may have seen only a part of the crime. You may not have seen anything. For example, you heard a loud noise, and you happened to look at your wrist watch and made a mental note of the time. Give an impartial account of that part of a crime which you witnessed.

Give an eye-witness account of a crime. (In this instance, you have seen everything, or nearly everything.) How do you feel as you tell the police your story? Are you afraid of reprisal on the part of the criminal? Are you relieved to be telling what you know?

Describe a rat; a squealer; a stool pigeon.

You are a police officer or detective. You are interrogating one of the following: a witness, a suspect, a stool pigeon, a known mobster. What questions do you ask and how do you ask them? How does the person being interrogated answer?

People involved in a crime sometimes meet to talk with one another. Arrange a meeting between: two suspects; a suspect and a witness; a suspect and a private eye; a witness and a private eye; a private eye and a police officer. (You might write the dialogue between all or some of the above. Have a crime in mind as you write the dialogue. Don't forget that meetings are usually arranged because people want something from one another; information, a promise of secrecy, protection.)

Imagine a room in your house in very exact detail, with all its colors, furniture and ornaments. You have just walked into the room. But something just doesn't seem right to you. You look all around. Then you realize that something is missing. What is it? (It can be anything at all.) How and why did you notice its absence? What did you do about it? Invent a character who stole the object. Describe her physical appearance and personality and make up a personal history for her. What was her motive in taking the object? Was the object important to you? To the criminal? Why? You may wish to tell how you found out the criminal. Invent some clues, witnesses and other suspects if you like. Write in the first-person singular if possible.

An object has been stolen or defaced. This object was of great value to you. Its value may have been monetary, but it also may have been sentimental. Tell why the object was important to you. Perhaps there is a story connected with it.

A crime has been committed. Write the interior monologue of the victim before, during and after the crime. Now write the interior monologue of the criminal covering the same time span. Do the two say anything to each other while the crime is going on?

What does a bank robber say to a bank teller? What does the robber say or do if the bank teller gives him a hard time?

You are a witness reviewing a police lineup. Whom are you looking for and why? Your recollection of the face of the criminal is uncertain. (What was the crime?) You look at face after face. What do the faces look like? What are your feelings and what goes through your mind as you look into each face? Suddenly you see the right face! How do you know that it is the right one? What do you say? Do? What does the person in the lineup say and do when he is identified?

There are many ways in which a criminal can be caught. You have caught the criminal you have been looking for.

How did you do it? Be specific when describing the events leading up to the capture and arrest.

You did it! You committed the crime! Now write your confession. Explain why you did it.

Have you ever kept a secret from someone? Did you keep it successfully, or did it leak out?

Imagine the secrets of: a young girl; a man sitting in a jail cell; a boy walking down the street holding a box in his hands; a person running through a house that is on fire; a husband; a wife; a jeweler; a banker; a white woman; a black woman.

What is your secret?

Like Sherlock Holmes, a detective may have a sidekick (Dr. Watson) and a nemesis (Moriarty). The sidekick goes with the detective on all the detective's exploits. Although he sees everything the detective sees, he does not draw conclusions; he is always a few steps behind the detective. The nemesis, however, is nearly the detective's intellectual equal and can occasionally outsmart him. You are a detective with a sidekick and a rival. What are your real feelings about these two?

Describe a detective from the viewpoint of his sidekick and his nemesis.

In order to write a mystery you must know your characters very well. Prepare a list of characters. Next to their names include any personality traits you can think of: routine upon waking, favorite foods, daily schedule, quirks and eccentricities, physical description, temperament, weaknesses, etc. You might, after completing this list, wish to assign certain characters on your list the roles of criminal, victim, suspect, witness, detective. You might try writing a story around the list.

Write the biography of a victim.

You are being blackmailed. Who is blackmailing you and why? What is your secret? Why do you wish to keep it a secret?

You are on trial for your life. You are awaiting the verdict. The jury has just returned. What thoughts are going through your mind? What are you feeling? The foreman of the jury says, "We have reached a verdict." What is the verdict? What is your reaction?

Write according to this skeleton story: A crime has been committed. Someone discovers it. A detective is hired. The detective listens to a few witnesses and questions a few suspects. He follows someone, and gets into trouble. He is captured, then escapes. He chases a suspect, catches him and wrests a confession from him. The detective goes home. (Try to include physical descriptions, pertinent facts, feelings of characters, settings of scenes, etc.)

More Mystery Games

Mystery games may be played in the class in several ways. To begin with, there can be a stolen object. It need not belong to a student. It should probably be owned by the class: a basketball, for example, or a papier-maché project that everyone is working on. The object may also belong to the teacher or the principal. Let the game proceed as in the story.

The teacher chooses one to five "criminals" whose job it is

116

to commit a crime—obviously not a major one but one related to the classroom. They would probably take and hide an object that would be missed at some point during the school day. Although the class would expect the crime to happen, no one who wasn't involved in it would know who the criminals were. The criminals must arrange to meet and commit the crime, perhaps during the lunch hour, probably with the teacher looking on. Since the other students would be anticipating a crime, a few might hang around the classroom and, who knows, maybe even witness the crime or part of it. When the theft is noticed by the rest of the class, all the students turn sleuths. They are responsible for questioning their classmates and getting them to account for their time. Suspects are those students who do not have satisfactory alibis. The criminals may offer alibis that are transparently false. They may insist, for example, that they were in the yard, although no one saw them, or a few may say that they were in the school library. The class sleuths need only check at the library to find out the truth. The stolen object may be hidden in the classroom. It may be found in the desk of one of the criminals or planted in an innocent student's desk. (The innocent student may expect to find it in his desk but still may not know the identity of the criminals.) A mysterious note may turn up. Perhaps it is a clue, in the form of a riddle, or a red herring (hardly cricket!). A simple clue might be a piece of clothing owned by one of the criminals and left at the scene of the crime: a glove or shoe that can be easily matched with its mate. Don't forget, though, that the easier the clues, the shorter the game. Search parties may be sent out to look for clues or for missing classmates posing as frightened witnesses. Basically the teacher is staging a play in the classroom. The students know that a play is going on, and they are participating in it. The teacher is the director.

Another variation on the idea of staged mysteries again involves the entire class, but in another way and with a different focus. Let one group of students write and plan a scene involving a criminal act. The group will perform the scene in pantomime before the rest of the class. The group ought to rehearse enough so that the scene can be done smoothly and repeatedly in precisely the same way, if necessary. Costumes are a nice addition. Gestures should be big, evocative, realistic. When the group presents its pantomime to the class, the rest of the students act as witnesses and sleuths. The pantomime should show how the crime was committed, against whom, and who witnessed it; it may even include the solution. The audience (witnesses and sleuths) can then write up versions of what they think they saw, including dialogue, characters' names, occupations, motives

behind the characters' actions. There should be as many versions as there are students in your class. The activity is in effect matching words to pictures.

Activities for the Teacher*

Place five or more objects on a table in front of your class. Let your students study them. They may include silly items like rubber ducks, practical items like pencils, exotic ones like black masks or shrunken heads. They should be evocative of different moods. Ask your students to close their eyes after they have studied the table for a while. While their eyes are closed, remove one or two items from the table. If there are many items (twenty or thirty, say), your students will enjoy guessing which ones are missing. Now ask your students to invent a thief. This may be done first as a story told by the group, then as pieces written by individual students. Who is the thief? What does she look like? Why

---

* These activities were based on or inspired by Total Effect, Resources for Education, an organization headed by Leonard Allison, Bob Perrault and Len Jenkin, and committed to teacher training.

does she steal the item? What was going through her mind as she stole it? Where is she taking it? You may also suggest that your students invent a place other than the real classroom and table from which it was stolen: for example, a rich man's living room, a palace, a gas station. Whom did this object belong to? What does the owner look like? What kind of personality does she have? How does she react when she discovers the theft? Does the object stolen have a special significance for her? For the thief?

If you are as sneaky as I am, inspect your students' coat pockets or desks when they're not around. (Get class permission first.) You'll probably find some interesting stuff. Remove the contents, or the most interesting contents, of one desk or coat pocket. Present these to the class and ask them to deduce whose they are. If they guess, make sure they tell you their reasons. A crumpled bag may lead someone to remember that she saw Joe eating potato chips in the yard at lunchtime. Gloves are a nice find, too. It has been my experience that students don't really mind this snooping, nor do they regard it as an invasion of privacy. They just think it is fun and feel particularly special if theirs are the pockets that have been picked.

Interrogation: think of a fictional character or a real person (Sherlock Holmes or the principal of your school) whom all your students are sure to be familiar with. What kinds of things will they need to know to guess his or her identity? They will need to know such things as, man or woman, young or old, real or fictional, color of hair, occupation, physical appearance, where the person lives, nationality, hobbies, religion, talents, birthplace, etc. Before letting the students ask about this person, make them categorize their questions: occupation, talents, sex, etc. Write the categories on the blackboard if only to impress the class with the variety of components involved. Explain to the students that these are the categories to which all their questions must relate. Then answer their questions, *but only with yes or no*. (You may decide to end the questioning if the class doesn't guess the identity of the person after twenty *no's*. The game often succeeds in turning the class into a group, all working together; sometimes it slows down or inhibits questioning or risk taking. The effect of this kind of pressure is itself an interesting theme for class discussion after the lesson.) Once you have led this game, your students may wish to lead it also.

Ask your students to walk around school, neighborhood or home with a note pad. Their activity is to spy. Yes, to spy. To jot down anything and everything they overhear. Their final piece may come out sounding like stream-of-consciousness writing, like a poem of sorts. It may even make sense. Your students can go from place to place to do their spying or can sit in one place, like the general office.

Ask your students to invent a crime, the criminal who committed it, and a motive to explain it. The motive should be fairly complex. Then ask them to devise an entirely different motive: why does the detective think the crime was committed? Now, assuming that all three explanations are correct, write, from the criminal's viewpoint, why he really did it.

Plan a visit to a museum with your students. A museum of natural history would be best for this activity. Let your students roam about the museum and pick one object they are particularly taken with. It may be an African mask, a statue, a musical instrument, a painting, a set of colonial glassware, a suit of armor. Because it is in a museum, the students know it is valuable, perhaps invaluable. Ask them to describe the object with care. Then ask them to place it in a different environment—an apartment, a mansion, an African hut. Who owns the object? Does it have a special meaning or worth for its owner? Is it cursed? One day it is stolen. Who is suspected of the theft and what are his motives? How and where is it finally found? Ask your students to tell the story behind the theft and rediscovery of the object. If there is a curse surrounding it, what happens to the thief after the object is stolen?

The Popular Love Story

Unlike other genres, the romance specializes in illustrating the movements people make toward one another. A romance depicts rhythms of human contact and interaction; how people meet, come together, move closer, move apart, separate, reunite, separate again, meet and so on. Every moving apart (due to distrust, jealousy, physical separations) is a test that love can overcome only if it is "true."

Most protagonists of romances have been women. For centuries love and marriage have been regarded as the culmination of women's lives, and a whole literature evolved to reflect this fact. Rarely are these romantic protagonists liberated characters, but rather fawning and selfless creatures whom many readers now find out of date and disturbing. A great deal could be said concerning women in the popular romance, but here, for obvious reasons, I'll concentrate on the fundamental elements of the genre.

First off, a romance often takes place in a romantic setting. Opinions and tastes may vary on what that is exactly, but often it's a place that is strange or new to the romantic protagonist. She may have come there to forget someone or something in her past. A Caribbean island, damp and foggy London, a house on a cliff overlooking the wild ocean: whatever the actual setting, it is less significant than the mood of loneliness and yearning for love it inspires in the central character.

The young woman is usually alone. She may make friends, but generally the other people she meets are very much different from her in interests, temperament, and sensitivity. They are not really her equals, nor do they deserve to be her confidants. (That role is reserved for the reader.) Instead, they serve as foils or opposites who make her seem all the more alone and deserving of love. The reader identifies with her, of course; to make identification easier, her personality is, in a word, ordinary. She must never be so unusual that our interest in her search for love takes second place to our interest in her personality.

The encounter between the woman and the man who is to be her lover is the first crucial action in a romance story. How do they meet? Is it love at first sight? Or does love evolve in less auspicious circumstances? In more sophisticated novels the first meeting is significant and reflects the essence of the future relationship. Lovers may be introduced through friends or meet by chance. One lover may come to the rescue of the other in a dangerous situation. The two might bump into each other, as they do in mouthwash commercials. Or a dramatic event may bring them together: for example, the shipwreck in the movie *The African Queen*.

Physical description is an essential. The reader must, at some point in the story, find the lover-to-be attractive. His features are drawn according to the presumed taste of the protagonist and the preferences of the writer and her audience. He is a kind of magnificent doll, whose face, hair and clothes we may arrange to suit ourselves. Underneath his outward appearance are both power and gentility.

As the protagonist's sole confidants, we hear her size him up. "How gentle he is!" or "What a hearty laugh he has!" We listen in as she considers his qualifications. The indispensable characteristic of the prospective lover is trustworthiness. Even the swarthy, moody heroes of gothic romances immediately inspire trust.

As the story progresses the protagonist finds out more about the man through experience or through what she hears from him or from other characters who know him. She may learn of a tragedy he suffered that impresses her and us with his courage and fortitude, or of his pride, sense of honor, generosity, etc. Our initial belief in him grows stronger. Like anxious parents, we begin to approve of him; he is right for our girl.

Later in the story overtures are made and accepted; affection is received and returned. The lovers declare their love, promise to be faithful, express fear of what may happen in the future, question each other closely.

The love relationship must then be tested. Various temptations arise and obstacles intrude. Jealous rivals, rumors, conflicts of will, arguments over money make the reader doubt the strength of the lovers' bond. In romances written for or by adolescents, parents inherit the role of villain. Usually they mean well, but because of their lack of understanding, overprotectiveness, or jealousy, they try to keep the lovers apart.

Will the couple's love survive? That is *the* romantic question. The protagonists undergo a series of tests: separation, temptation, infidelity, anger, jealousy, distrust. No matter how often they lose each other, in the end love prevails. The couple wins the right to stay together. In the final scene, which often takes place in another romantic setting, avowals of love are sealed by a kiss, a proposal, a wedding or, nowadays, by the sex act.

Physical closeness is crucial to these stories, especially when they are written for young people who within a few years will be kissing and petting for the first time. They are looking forward to the experience, and these scenes—brief, evocative and innocent—help them in a small way to prepare themselves.

Words such as "gentle," "tender," "warm," portray physical closeness as soft and sweet. These descriptive passages, for the young reader or writer, are the most powerful in the story. They are what one writes and reads such stories for.

A love story may convey feelings of loneliness, yearning, sexual attraction, betrayal, exaltation, fulfillment. Fear and anger may be expressed in any genre, but only in romance are they connected to closeness between people. A romance is the history of a relationship and of all the feelings associated with it.

Different Strokes for
Different Folks: Four Classes

Emotional and physical needs are not the easiest things for our students, or us, to write about. Although romance is the most difficult of all the genres, and can be tricky to work with, it is also probably the most revealing and personally rewarding.

When is your class ready to write a romance? Students from the first grade to college have worked in this genre. Age is not the determining factor. Very young children have crushes, think about getting married and having babies. They are aware of the difference between boys and girls. They already know something about the romance between their mothers and fathers:

How do you feel between boys and girls?
I feel that boys are good to use for working.
If we had no girl there would be no people.

— Mary Margaret Dolan

My father was married to another woman and my mother was

128

married to another man and they both got a divorce from the other man and woman and a friend of my mother and father one day on the beach met them both and introduced them and they got married.

—Conor McCort

Well, my mother said to me when she was little she do not know nothing about the man and woman in love. So then she said, You know anything about the man and woman in love? So I said, Mother, when you was little you do not know the man and woman in love well I do.

—Wong Mo

Young students also have an understanding of platonic love:

I remember
when my friend
broke her arm
It touched something
deep inside
her eyes flooded with tears
I hated that

—Neal Giarro

Children are attracted to members of the opposite sex, admire them, even experience crushes:

You are the nicest girl in the class—at least the second nicest girl in the class.

—Kim Brantley

I like this person who plays hard to get. The person is in this class. The person has a sister too. I like her but she plays hard to get too.

—Curtis Ortiz

Sometimes their feelings seem uncontrollable and disturbing. They produce all shades of shame and guilt:

DIRT IN YOUR MIND
Did you ever get that dirty feeling
You feel like a piece of garbage
So you go home and take a bath
Then you find out it was only in your mind.

           —Demetrius Pellicier

To first-graders through third-graders, love stories are usually about getting married and having babies. The same themes when treated by older students are more fleshed out and more expressive of feelings.

Classroom romance need not precede a romance project. Giggling, note passing, teasing between sexes, are not prerequisites. Interest in the opposite sex is usually exhibited by a few students but felt in one way or another by the entire class. Others may feel envious or infringed upon. It would be rare indeed to find a class where everyone shared the same interests. Not every child likes reading or sports, or geography, but all are exposed to them. Should you expose an entire class to the writing of romances, too? You, the teacher, are the only one who can decide whether you ought to embark upon a romance project.

In my attempts to teach romance and romance writing, I have never failed to collect stories from a class. Some students resisted writing romances; where I felt the resistance stemmed from a genuine threat, I gave the student another assignment unrelated to romance. Some students, although willing to try romance, simply don't relate to the genre. One student of mine, whom I referred to earlier, wrote a three-page story about a plane hijacking in which the only element of romance was a honeymooning couple among the passengers. He had intended to write a romance, but his imagination led him into an adventure story.

Not all writing assignments need to be taken up by the whole class. Certain themes can better be handled in smaller groups, or even on an individual basis. There are as many ways to teach the romance story as there are classes or groups. I'd like to describe a few approaches to the teaching of this genre and tell how a romance project was received in four different groups.

I

Gina and Michael were two among ten children who met for a summer writing workshop at a local Brooklyn library. In the winter they and the rest of the group attended a parochial school. Gina was blond, pretty, mischievous and very provocative sexually. She was tomboyish, sturdy but ultrafeminine with her pastel hair clips and her painted fingernails. She always brought a friend or a following to group. She was a star.

Michael, going on thirteen, was small for his age. He had a slight but perceptible nervous tic, his face and eye twitched, he spoke nasally and too fast. He was very active in sports; his favorite kind of writing was a fast-paced description of sporting events that he had witnessed. His friends, all much bigger than he, ribbed him about participating in the group. They would occasionally show up outside the glass door to our room and point in and laugh. Michael took this good-naturedly, and laughed too. He was at the workshop because he liked writing. Most of the others came because it gave them something to do and because the sessions were held in an air-conditioned room during a very hot city summer. It seemed to me that at least one reason why Gina came was to be near Michael.

For the first few weeks, the rest of the group had revolved around these two. The others, all girls, were quiet, well behaved, perhaps a little shocked, as well as entertained, at the seductive lengths to which Gina would go, poking Michael, teasing him, chasing him, hitting him, sticking her tongue out at him, performing stunts and staging scenes to

131

get his attention. Sometimes the sessions were like watching nine women stranded on an island with only one man. By mutual consent, and owing to the shyness of the other girls, Gina was the queen bee.

Michael responded to her flirtations somewhat sheepishly. He enjoyed the attention, but it embarrassed him, too, and he often resorted to calling her "stupid" and "a baby," and told her to "shut up."

The other eight girls participated in this romantic drama by watching it. They were an engrossed, and no doubt envious, audience.

All the children had been subjected to discipline in their tightly structured classes and in their homes. In situations where discipline was relaxed, as in our writing workshop, they were apt, like freed animals, to let loose.

I had been having the group write in genre. I had taught a two-year project through Teachers & Writers Collaborative based on genre and was at work on this book. The group had already had a taste of writing horror stories, mysteries and adventures. Should I, I wondered, introduce them to the romance? It was the one genre that most clearly paralleled the group experience. Should I offer them a means of expressing what was apparently going on inside them? Would it exacerbate what was already happening? If so, would that be bad? Would it provide too much stimulation for Gina? Would it offend and alienate the rest of the group by making their role as outsiders more obvious and perhaps more painful?

We were sitting around during the third session. They had sampled almost every genre. "What's next?" one of them asked. I decided to take them into my confidence, to let them make the decision.

"Well, I was thinking about writing a romance, but I don't know if you're into that." It was clear to them that there were other writing ideas we could try if this one made them too uncomfortable.

Gina was giggling already and popping out of her seat. The girls watched her. She would hit Michael's head, then jump away, hit and jump, hit and jump. She was daring him to play a game of tag with her. Finally provoked, he chased her around the room. She squealed and screamed. The others looked on dumbly, enviously, breaking into laughter finally when Michael caught her, pulled her arms behind her and squeezed her thin body in the most ambivalent hug imaginable. The other girls ran over as if to protect her. Michael was caught more than ever between disapproval and enjoyment of Gina's antics.

Oh oh, I thought, I'm sinking in over my head. My fear of losing control at that moment was intense. I was beginning to imagine myself as some sort of pervert-instigator of children's doctor games. I gulped. Was this what I was hired for? They were all acting crazy now, out of their seats and dashing around the room. If I didn't channel their energy, it might turn on itself, and I could really be in hot water.

"Well, I see that this idea interests you, so let's begin." I jumped in, hurriedly passing out paper and pencils. But I soon saw that they weren't into private writing. They were involved with telling a story among themselves, embroidering details, and joking and giggling. The pencils were superfluous. The story had already started.

"All right," I said, "I'll be your secretary. You can *all* tell the story together and I'll write down whatever you say. But nothing too sexy," I warned them, "because that's private and it wouldn't be cool in this situation." God only knows what they thought I meant by "this situation." If they had asked me I would have probably explained that if kids want to talk sexy with friends it is a private affair in which adults shouldn't really take part.

But they didn't ask. They just continued telling their story. I responded seriously and respectfully to the story they had already started, asking them to repeat what I had missed so that I could take it down. The whole activity must

133

have been over in twenty minutes. There was a lot more giggling along with some of the usual disorder of children out of their seats, hanging over my shoulder to make sure the story got written down correctly. The group remembers this session as the "funniest" they had with me. And that counts for something.

Were they overstimulated by this activity? Weren't they already overstimulated by their own activity? Out of some added consciousness brought to bear on the situation by an adult these children were able to produce a story reflecting an emotional undercurrent in their own lives.

The story they wrote juxtaposes popular love phrases and images and reads somewhat like a poem. To an adult reader the sexuality may seem overt (not to mention rampant), a combination of the repressed and the outrageous. To children it is just a very silly and very funny story.

"I love you, dear," said Steven to Connie.
"I love you too." They were in the forest, sitting on
a log, kissing. Ah, refreshing.
"Let us be married at once!"
"Oh shut up you dirty pig!"
Just then he grabbed her and she smacked him. He shot her
with a gun.
"I'm all wet!" said Connie, "from that water gun."
"You mushy dame!"
"I can't get over you."
"When do we get our divorce?"
"When do we get married?"
They left the forest and they went to the guy's apartment.
"Let's have a duel. Let's squirt each other with water guns."
And that's what they did. After they were all wet, they went
to a costume party. One dressed like Cinderella, the other
like a prince.

II

Early on in my teaching of genre, I was working with a group of girls who, although they were not friends, shared a common love for Beverly Cleary books. Worn copies of *Fifteen* circulated among them. They pored over such works as *Janie's First Carnation* and *Bunnie's Big Date*.

Most of these girls did not know me. I had never worked with them before. Their trust in me was limited, and since I had just begun teaching genre I, too, proceeded cautiously. I could not ask them point blank if they had romantic interests. Such a question might have offended them and made them feel uncomfortable. There was no direct way into this group's experience. They were already called the "Romance Group" and that was probably difficult enough to admit to classmates, teachers and themselves. I could not ask them to write from experience. Instead I decided to use literary models as an entrance into the genre.

I began with such classic adult literature as *Anna Karenina*, picking scenes and bits of dialogue or description that my students might discuss or imitate, and adding on to them new beginnings or endings.

I read, for example, a description of Vronsky as he glanced slyly at Anna. For contrast, I read a description of Anna's dull husband. We discussed the effect of both passages. They were attracted to Vronsky but distrustful of him: "a serene smile that showed his even teeth." They disliked Anna's husband altogether: "He is not a man but a machine, a spiteful machine when he is angry." I asked such questions as: Did you ever know someone you liked but distrusted? Someone you thought was cute but untrustworthy? How does a "spiteful machine" walk? Eat? Talk? How does he kiss his children good morning or goodbye? His wife?

I would base writing assignments on these discussions. Using the idea of fatal attraction (again from *Anna Karenina*), I asked them to write stories in which they had to choose between someone or something safe but boring, and someone or something exciting but dangerous. We also talked and wrote about irresistible urges: eating too much, watching TV when mother isn't home even though she has forbidden you, etc. These ideas did not necessarily have to be explored in terms of physical urges: they applied to other, less loaded areas of their everyday lives.

Working from literary segments has its drawbacks, however; although it does produce writing ideas, it fails to bring to students the sense of a complete story, its conventions and plot. Since my sixth-grade students couldn't possibly read *Anna Karenina* or *Camille*, I summarized these novels, giving their skeletons, or bare plots. But this was hardly the same as exposing students to complete stories, for here it was not they but I who was actually experiencing the story and dissecting it. I wanted *them* to discover story patterns. For this purpose the classics were too long; if I predigested them, the students were too dependent on me.

So I switched to shorter books, to more accessible popular romances. I assigned the girls the adolescent love stories that they were already so fond of. Working with these books, they were able to analyze the kinds of things that took place in a romance story: the "elements" of the genre.

But how could I get them to write their own stories? The group moved into this next phase by itself. One session I was reading to them from one of the Harlequin Romances. These books are sold in five-and-dimes and are full of adolescent crushes and hand-holding idylls. I chose a story about a young girl who awakes blissfully happy on her wedding day only to receive a telegram from her betrothed breaking their engagement. I intended to ask the group to take the character's place and write the end of the story.

The girls were impatient for me to finish reading. They were critical of the story, complaining that it was not romantic enough. When I asked them how they would change it, they told me in great detail, with an expertise that really impressed me. I put the book down and asked them to write what *they* considered a good romance story. The project had taken a new turn.

I wondered whether literary models had been necessary other than as a means of getting started. These girls contained within themselves all the love stories that have ever been or will ever be. They were completely at home in the conventions of romance.

III

Class 4-5-6-324 had a friendly and open atmosphere. The teacher allowed a good deal of freedom. She was sometimes upset at the class's inability or refusal to complete projects or to progress more rapidly in academic subjects. It was an energetic class, and although hard to harness and teach, the students related unusually well to one another. They had a genuine interest in one another uncommon in most classrooms. The teacher's influence was obvious here. She held frequent class discussions in which social and personal issues were discussed. Whenever a conflict between students or student and teacher arose, it was brought up at these meetings. Ms. Finder took pride in her sensitivity to her students; she kept close tabs on their feelings.

I had taught horror, mystery and adventure to this class, coming in once a week, presenting a lesson or discussion and finally an idea for writing. The class had responded enthusiastically, and just about everyone wrote.

When I suggested to Ms. Finder that we try the romance genre next, she smiled knowingly. That seemed a very satisfactory idea because she believed that a benign cupid had already shot a few arrows into her classroom. Everyone was so close and friendly in her class that it seemed bound to happen. She described it as a mild, innocent case of spring fever—a little comical, nothing serious. Romance stories would be fun and very topical.

I began my spiel: "We've written many different kinds of stories, and today I thought we'd try a new type: romance."

Neither Ms. Finder nor I had understood the lengths to which cupid had gone. Crushes and young loves came crawling out of the woodwork! At the very mention of the word "romance," the students grew excited, nervous, giggly and red-faced. They left their seats, pointed at one another. Both the teacher and I were amazed at this sudden eruption. The room was filled with shouts, protestations and denials of love. The intensity of their interest in one another was mind-boggling. Their young affairs had surfaced at the slightest provocation; a single word had sent them haywire.

This was delicate ground. How to traverse it? Better take a good look at the lay of the land. How could I ask this group of people to answer such questions as "How does a love story make you feel?" or "What kinds of things happen in a love story?" Such questions would only seem formal, beside the point and silly compared to their immediate experience, which was going on right before my eyes. In order for them to feel such crushes they had to be having various romantic fantasies. Where there are fantasies there are stories. This class was a gold mine of stories. I decided to do some digging.

"You already seem to know about romance. Why don't you just write some stories? They can be real or made up. They can also be about a wish you have."

If you are faced with the kind of obvious and rampant energy that I found in Ms. Finder's class, and in my library group, your best bet is to face it head on. Assume that in order to have achieved this degree of feeling they have had to have experienced fantasies. Whether conscious or not, these narrative undercurrents are your best and most vibrant sources of good, enthusiastic writing. Try not to seem embarrassed by your students' display of romantic interest in one another. If you are embarrassed, face your class head on anyway. Try to get them right into the act of writing a romance, individually or in a group. You may not need to introduce the subject, explore or discuss it. Your students' actions and responses may be introduction enough.

And don't forget: a piece may seem corny to you yet have contained electricity for your student during the act of writing. (This is especially common with romances.) Sometimes the intensity of the writing experience is more important than the final product.

IV

Not every group or class finds the subject of romance funny or titillating. Ms. Betts's fifth-grade and sixth-grade class, for example, was very sophisticated. The class was racially and ethnically mixed, with no one group predominant. Though not brilliant, the students, partly owing to the teacher's influence, were mature, independent, self-possessed. Some were street-wise, some were book-read, others were psychologically advanced, still others were highly motivated academically and generally. Ms. Betts ran her class for thirty-five individuals, all of whom knew that a straight question would receive a straight answer. I could have a reasonably sophisticated conversation with nearly every child in the room. Very few responded shyly or coyly. Most were opinionated and expressive. They certainly were not perfectly behaved, and there were the usual displays of loud talking, arguments, contests of wills between students and students and teacher.

Many of the students in the class were popular around school. Others looked up to them, followed them, had crushes on them. They would be dating within a year, if they weren't already. These popular students did not openly set the tone of the class, but their mature sociability was observed and definitely admired.

I had planned to teach romance through the building-up method. The group zipped through qualities and gave in fifteen minutes what had taken other classes an hour. They were moving just as quickly through elements. The subject of sex came out immediately, but it was a foregone conclusion that this was part of romance, and it hardly drew a laugh.

Then they stumbled on the one element that fascinated them: the meeting of boy and girl. The questions, answers and discussion that followed centered on the how and why of physical attraction. The students were absorbed by *beginnings*. This seems reasonable, doesn't it? They themselves were on the threshold of romance, and here was an opportunity to pick up some practical information as well as to share fantasies and compare notes with one another. Ms. Betts and I added very little to the discussion; we were needed only to recognize raised hands and to keep monologues to a minimum.

What attracts people to one another? Money, physical appearance, sex. Some subtler possibilities also came up; a strong person might be attracted to a weaker one; a cruel person might be attracted to a kind one; a depressed, serious person to a happy optimist. They seemed to be suggesting, I pointed out, that opposites attract.

Where did people meet, and how? Formal introductions, pick-ups, chance meetings in bars, stores, parks, streets. They began considering such situations as two passengers getting stuck in an elevator together, a janitor fixing a tenant's radiator, etc. I felt that now they had some stories on their minds. They fell right into telling romances, the emphasis still on boy meets girl.

The class did not write stories that day. The lesson had been long and exciting, and they had worked hard. They seemed to have gotten something genuine, almost practical, out of their discussion. The class had not covered all the specifics of the romance genre, but they did cover in depth the one that most interested them. I would have been working against myself if I had tried to turn them in another direction. The stories they told aloud reflected the variety of possibilities in the genre.

When I returned the next week, I asked the class to write a romance. The results were very satisfactory. In the time between lessons, elements other than boy meets girl had somehow gotten absorbed into their stories. Nonetheless, what had interested them foremost in reality took the most prominent place in their writing.

Romance for Boys

Romance is commonly thought of as a feminine interest. Even this book presents a chapter focused on the romantic fantasies of twelve-year-olds. Boys and men rarely if ever turn the TV to a love movie, or pick a Beverly Cleary off the book shelf. Because the genre is thought of as girlish, some boys may be squeamish about trying to write a romance. As they get older, because they have more experience, they are far more willing to try their hand. Read, for example, some of the romances written by male college students; almost all are based on real-life experience. Interestingly, this fact does not make their fantasies seem any more realistic.

But why wait until your male students are older? Some of the most moving love stories I have collected were written by boys twelve or younger. It all depends on the teacher's and students' willingness to take risks.

Generally speaking, it is true that girls start losing sleep over their romantic inclinations sooner than do boys. If you find that your male students are less willing and less equipped to write romances, you shouldn't necessarily push them. You may, however, be able at least to introduce them to the genre through lectures and class discussions and so expose them to a kind of story with which they are not so familiar.

If we ask girls to write in genres that are typically considered masculine (horror, mystery, adventure), why shouldn't we also ask boys to experiment with romance? Are boys' romantic fantasies so different from girls'? These points are certainly well worth class discussion.

The Feeling You Get

You can love other things besides girl,
Love is more important than, than well
I really don't know how to explain it, it's
like a disease.

—Demetrius Pellicier

To My Girl

I love you as much as I love my mother
and sometimes more. I love you for your
face and for your skin and your eyes and
your body.

—Derrick Knowles

A Person Looking Across The Room

I always stare at a girl across the room I always stare at her
maybe because she's the girl I like the best in the class I don't

know why. But maybe she's got something I like in girls because all the girls I've liked are the same way but some aren't that quiet but I guess it's alright. What I like in girls is they're pretty, nice quiet, but not that much and I don't like girls that are too fresh. And the girl I stare at has all those things that I like. But it's a shame I am not going to see her again. I am leaving in 2 days. It's a shame because we could have become good friends.

—Alex Matos

The Romantic Lives
of Twelve-Year-Old-Girls

The stories that follow were written by girls aged ten to twelve, members of a group that met once a week for two years for the express purpose of writing romances. Boys were excluded at the girls' request. They wanted privacy and freedom to let go without fear or embarrassment. (Revealing these romantic fantasies to one another caused enough discomfort and self-consciousness.) The members were daughters of the white middle class and of the black and Puerto Rican upwardly mobile lower middle class. About forty girls passed through this group, twenty of them staunch regulars. As their writing teacher, I never attempted consciousness raising, although these stories suggest a fertile and ready field for it; rather, I provided an outlet for loneliness and repressed sexual feelings.

At no other time in a woman's life is fantasy so crucial as it is at puberty. The twelve-year-old must of necessity spend a large part of time in her fantasy life: she is driven into it. Her position is a lonely one. The body is willing, but the boys

145

are not. Her crushes almost always come to naught. Her male classmates are still too busy playing: "Tommy was a boy every girl admired in class. He was tall and acting like just the other boys: plain and childish." Crushes may last for years and be carried like baggage from grade to grade.

The story you are about to read is true. The names have been changed to protect the innocent. When my friend was in the third grade (my friend is two years older than me) she met a boy named Jonathan. He was new to the school. When he first came she hated him. But after a week they were talking about things like old friends. And when summer that year came she only thought of him. When the fourth grade finally came he was there. This year they had to be separated because their math teacher said they couldn't concentrate in the same class.

When fourth grade Christmas vacation came they missed each other a lot. My friend wanted him to come over but couldn't get up the nerve to ask him and they talked to each other after school. In the fifth grade he wasn't coming to her school anymore. She cried. She hasn't forgot him yet.

—(name withheld)

David hits me. And sometimes when I get home I call him on the telephone. His phone number is ***-****. And he don't like me and I call him because I like him. And when he was fussing at me Miss Brayboy says, "Stop it David." And sometimes I call him and his mother says that he don't be home. Sometimes I be thinking that he is home. Then the next day when I came home at 3 o'clock, my cousin came over named Sandy, and I gave her David's phone number. So David spoke to my cousin. So Sandy asked him: "Do you like Wanda?"

And David said: "I can't stand her guts! I can't stand her guts! I can't stand her guts!"

So Sandy said: "Hold it a minute David. Do you like Yolanda?"

And he said: "Nah. Nah."

So the next day in class Miss Brayboy said: "How come you're hitting Wanda?"

"Because Wanda hit me first."

He got me at the yard and I told Miss Brayboy. Then after 3
o'clock I hit him I hit him I hit him I hit him.

—Wanda

In frustration she may turn to older boys in junior high
school. She may mope over strangers in the street, models in
magazines, singers or TV stars. But again, with these strangers
loved from afar, the situation is hopeless. She is stuck,
probably for the first time, with loneliness: she is experiencing her first stirrings of separateness. Later in her life this
should be her main source of strength, but for the moment
she experiences only the blues, attacks of aloneness for which
the only known cure is boys. Or thinking about them.

He was cute, good in all his subjects, and nice. Every time I
saw him I could feel my heart doing weird things. I tried to act
cool, while inside my stomach the butterflies were multiplying by
the seconds.

I looked into his face, a bit chubby, and not *really* that
handsome. It's mainly his personality that I like. True love? I
have had many crushes and each one felt deeper than the one
before. Each time I say to myself, "I'll never get over this crush,
the others were different. Tomorrow when I wake up I'll
probably find someone new." But deep inside I think that I'm
lying to myself.

—Sarah

But in most cases boys are unobtainable, so girls look to
girls, with whom they can have real relationships. They form
groups in which there is frequent discussion of boys and sex.
Within these cliques I have witnessed intense conflict, the
point of which is to secure the "best girl" as one's best
friend. The strategy used is to point out the strangeness, or
separateness, of the other girls, while attributing greater
virtues to oneself.

I don't like Lisa because she always double crosses people and
she convinced Nina to pick on me and gang up on me. Then she

got all the boys together and all the girls and got them to bother me and call me names, like I was some sort of weirdo and they teased me about the way I dress. Then the next day when I came in with candy, she was my best friend. She's a rat.

—Eileen

Rejected by boys, girls turn to one another to act out dramas of triangles and preferred partners. Yet everyone fails the average sixth-grade girl because no one satisfies those lonely feelings that keep emerging all the time. Inevitably, she is driven into herself, and this is where romantic fantasy comes in: yearning for the great love who will end her loneliness.

She was sitting on the train once and she met a boy who she happened to like. He was sitting right next to her. He looked at her and she looked at him. It was his stop. He got off.

When he got off, she had that feeling that she should have talked to him, now that she didn't talk to him. She said to herself, "I'll never know his name or where he lives. That could have been the beginning of a good friendship," with tears in her eyes and a sigh of loneliness.

Then it came to her stop. As she was walking home, she was trying to imagine she saw him again, and she said to herself, "If I ever saw him again, I would ask him his name and address, and try to get to know him." But then she thought, "If I ever saw him again I probably wouldn't recognize him. Well, I guess I'm still alone and very lonely."

—Faith

There is a kind of heroics to the loneliness of these girls, in their ability to endure painful love songs on the radio and teasing thoughts of boys they cannot have or find. As lonely "romantics," they live in a state of readiness and receptivity in which anything is possible; around every corner, in every subway a prince may await. When a girl finally meets her one-and-only-forever-after, it seems as though fate has touched her.

Superficially, one might imagine these 1970's girls have the stamina to be alone; their appearance seems so non-conforming, so self-confident. They are freer in dress than we were, sturdier and less frilly in their dungarees and workboots. Pastel colors and hair ribbons have given way to bold colors and comfort. They seem to have thrown over any imposed image of girlhood. One would presume that this less trained image of femaleness would result in a far greater acceptance of themselves than past generations of young women experienced. Not so.

I have yet to read a girl describe herself in one of these stories without reservations. Each is highly critical of, or dissatisfied with, the shape of her body, her skin, her legs, even her voice. This wish for physical perfection is mainly attributable to her wanting to attract boys, particularly the ideal boy. In the absence of real boyrfriends, every girl in the romance group had invented one of the ideal variety. No wonder she believes she falls so short. After all, who else would the perfect boy be attracted to but the perfect girl? As soon as thoughts of the ideal boy surface, self-esteem sinks.

> At night I think of the Ideal Boy. I think of things like who is he? What does he look like? What is his name? Where will I meet him? How will I meet him? That's really all I think of at night. As of now I haven't met him yet. I forgot a few things before, but now I remember, so here they are: Where will we go on our first date? How tall is he? How handsome will he be? I'll never get him though. My hair's too ugly and disagreeable. My stomach is too fat and my legs are too long.
>
> —Laurie

> When I go to bed at night I think of boys, especially Mark. I think if I was skinny and beautiful, Mark would love me. I think of Mark's adorable face. Then all of a sudden I am thinking of Freddie Prinze. How adorable he is, I think. Then I think if Mark would like me for my looks and not my personality, he's awful! Then I get steaming mad at Mark and I make an imaginary boy. He's gorgeous. (In my thought I am, too.) We talk about nice

things and he loves me for my personality—not my body. His name is David, and I love him. There is a real David like this, and my imaginary David is like him in a few ways.

I hate my:

Stomach	Why?	Too fat.
Legs	Why?	Too fat.
Chin	Why?	Too fat.
Face	Why?	Too many blackheads.
Feet	Why?	They stink.
Hair	Why?	Never looks brushed even though I do.

—Ellen

I look at myself in the mirror.
I am beautiful.
But do you think so?
It's your opinion that matters.
I dab some lipstick on and walk
outside. There you are, a handsome brute.
Suddenly we are dancing.
I'm floating across the floor . . .
It's all over. The night was much too
short for me.

—Tanya

And how does one meet the ideal boy, but through an ideal opportunity. Love is still right around the corner. The girls thrived on love at first sight, part of what I have come to identify as the Big Bang theory in which love may strike at any moment, particularly when least expected. In fact, I never received a story about an unfolding relationship; love just hit a girl smack in the face and stayed for good. The group's basic concept of a romance story was as follows: love at first sight, a date, a kiss, marriage, children. The characters of these stories meet their lovers on the street, in subways and always by chance. "Just then a boy appeared" is a common introduction of many a male character. Very often he appears on the scene to come to a girl's aid.

150

One day I was walking down the street and I crashed into this boy. I said to myself, He is cute. I told my friend, and my friend said, "Yes, he is cute."

"By the way, what is your name?"

"My name is Rory."

And I told him my name, "My name is Ana."

So then he left and I said goodbye. Then me and my friend were talking to each other and I said to my friend, "He is my boyfriend."

—Ana

Teenage Joanne Jackson was walking to the store, for today was her birthday. Her mother gave her $10.00 for her to go shopping. She lost her money and started to cry. Starting back home, a boy appeared. He said, "Why are you crying?" She said, "I lost $10.00." "No need to cry," said he, "I found it."

—Doreen

But once a girl has a lover, just how much should she love him and how much should she let herself be loved? When it came to closeness with the opposite sex, the girls seemed threatened, afraid of losing a self that they had only recently discovered.

THE COFFEE SHOP

Marion sipped her hot coffee sitting in a restaurant booth alone. She did not see the figure standing beside her.

"May I join you?" he asked.

Marion turned around. "Of course."

He was tall, dark eyed and extremely handsome, she figured. She noticed how low he had buttoned his shirt.

"My name's Justin Barnes. Perhaps you never noticed me. I play the oboe in music class. Pretty lousy though," Justin said with a grin as he stared into Marion's eyes.

"Sorry. My name's Marion. Marion Lase."

"Are you French? Marion Lase sounds like a French name. French names like yours are beautiful," he told her as he kept

151

looking into her eyes.

"It is French. My father is French, and my mother is an American," she answered.

When they came out from the coffee shoppe, there was something different about them. They walked out hand-in-hand.

Justin gave Marion a lift home. He then said to her, "I'd like to see you tomorrow. Dinner, maybe? My treat."

"I'd love to!" Marion replied.

"Great. Pick you up at 8:00," Justin told her and left her without her objecting. Marion sighed. It was a soft sigh, with a fragrance of love about it. It was her first dinner date. She was 18, and never met a boy who made her smile so. Perhaps it was true. Maybe she was in love. She was sure it wasn't infatuation.

At 8:00 the next day, Justin arrived in his blue Chevy promptly. He took Marion to an unfancy but delicious restaurant. While they were at the table, comfortably seated, Marion asked him a question.

"How old are you Justin?"

He laughed. "Well, part of me is 80, my heart is 20, and my brain is 4."

Marion grinned. "No, really."

He lifted his eyebrows slowly. "Twenty. Why?"

"Oh," she answered. "I'm just curious."

They had dinner and patted their stomachs. Justin looked firmly into Marion's face. It wasn't a look, but it was a stare. And his lips were not turned up or down. Marion noticed how serious he looked, and she was almost about to laugh. But she didn't, as he started to speak in a low voice.

"Do you love me?" he asked, placing his hand in hers, studying her carefully. He watched how she crossed her legs, and held her fork in her slender, long polished fingers. Her eyes opened showing off her long lashes. Her hair fell before her ears, but Marion didn't bother to push it back. She was startled at Justin's question and didn't know what to say. She knew whatever she said would probably be stupid.

"Well, yes, I guess I do, Justin," and found nothing else to say but to wait for Justin's reply. He didn't say anything, so Marion spoke again.

"But after all, we just met."

Justin took his hand off hers, and ran his fingers through his hair.

"Even so, Marion," he began, "I feel a sort of 'thing' for you. I've always loved you, even before you knew me. I'd see you at lunch with your girlfriends, and I followed you to the coffee shoppe when you were alone, so I could get a chance to talk to you."

Marion shivered. She thought to herself, "This guy's really got something over me. He's making me feel creepy. And I mean I'm really getting the shivers. I love him, but I'm scared to love him, really."

When they were driving home, Marion noticed that this was not the way.

"Justin, are you heading for the park?" she asked suspiciously.

"It's the best way to see the moonlight," he answered. He then stopped the car in front of the park. "When I said 'I love you' I meant it. Now that we're even, it shouldn't be too hard to . . ." he said and stopped. He reached over to kiss her, but Marion backed away. "Please, Justin, don't!" she cried. But he couldn't be stopped. Marion jumped out of the car and took the bus home. There she cried for hours.

The next day, he was nowhere to be found. But there was someone at the counter. Marion. She sipped her hot coffee in the coffee shoppe. And somehow, she felt two eyes perplexed on her.

—Cece Lee

Who can tell the power and sway Justin will have over Marion when, in the future, his demands will no doubt begin all over again. This story expresses not only a fear of sex, but also a fear of closeness. Marion is very uncertain that she will be able to defend herself against masculine expectation and demand. Boys and men were viewed by most girls as superior, dominant animals, strange beings who are to be suspected, if not feared. Their stories, reflecting the familiar need to be protected, rescued, cherished, overwhelmed, and destroyed, suggest that they will have the same false and inevitably disappointing expectations of men as daughters of previous generations had.

One of the most common plots I received was that of the invasion story, in which a threatening man enters a woman's private terrain or personal space. He is up to no good and intends to rob or harm her. She is physically defenseless, but her innocence melts him. He confesses and repents, and they fall in love. There are many variations on this popular theme.

It was 10:00 at night and the window opened. In came a dark figure with a kind of bag over his shoulder. He walked all around the room. But then he heard a sound, it went *CLICK*! And the light turned on. There in the light stood a young girl. Blond hair, blue eyes, and in a nightgown. The girl started to scream. But the man calmed her down and started to explain.

The man and the lady sat down and drank hot cocoa. "My name is Sam, Sam Corey. I'm sorry what happened. Go and call the police, I don't care. I deserve it." "Why? Oh! My name is Linda Martin." "Because I tried to rob you!" "Well, I'm not going to the fuzz." "Thanks."

After they drank their hot cocoa, they turned on the record player and started to dance.

—Elizabeth

As Jane Smith was going home one day, she noticed someone seemed to be following her. So she decided to take a short cut through an alley. This was the wrong thing to do. Little did she know the person that was following her had escaped from an asylum. This person was a man; clever, sneaky, terribly crazy, and most of all, lonely.

He trapped her into a corner. He was just about to kill her. Suddenly, in a meek voice, she said, "Why are you doing this to me?" Slowly, he released his hand from her neck. The killer stared into the sky. Jane, being a warm and understanding person, began to talk to him. She found out that he was really a very warm, understanding person, too. Out of this, one thing led to another and, well, they fell in love.

—Donna

There were just two people on the train one day. They were just staring at each other until finally someone's stop came. The

154

lady got off. The man got off, too. They walked a little distance. Finally, she got in the street and she walked to her apartment. He walked, too.

She walked up to the second floor to her apartment. He walked, too, and he walked with his eyes wide open and on his face was a look of love.

She opened her door and went in. She locked the door with a double lock. When she saw him outside she sat down in her living room very scared. She stared like she was in shock. She didn't know that he loved her. She thought that he was out to kill her.

So finally there was a knock on the door. She walked slowly to the door. She said, "Yes, who is it?"

"It's me," he said.

"Who are you?"

"Just open the door."

So she unlocked the door and let him in.

—Faith

The power of some male characters over their women is evident in the following story:

One day Martha was walking out of the Riverside Theater. She met this boy named Bob. They talked like it was love at first sight. Everything went well till one day Martha had cancer.

Bob was seeing her a lot. She had to stay in the hospital for four months. She lasted one year in the hospital.

Bob gave up on waiting, so he left her. One month later her cancer was cured.

When she left she asked where her boyfriend was. The nurse said he left. So she went home. He wasn't there. She checked the parks and he wasn't there. She went home. And to her surprise he was home all right, but with another girl. Right then and there she had a heart attack.

Bob didn't even go to her funeral.

—Stephanie

The girls are afraid of being hurt and overwhelmed, but they are nonetheless interested in being pursued and seduced. Although they are far more aggressive than boys in their everyday romantic ventures, they are convinced that it should be the other way around. So, in most of their stories, the female characters are the sought-after recipients of devotion and affection. Men are the unlucky ones who must do without the women they love.

One day I was walking down the street to take the train to my friend's house, and I saw this beautiful, beautiful boy on the train. I was looking kind of good, and he said, "Hey, you're looking fine."

I didn't say anything, so I got on the train and went to my friend's house, and I told her what happened.

The next day I went to school and I saw him. He started talking to me, and I talked back to him, and me and him got together. I got to know him much better, and he asked me over to his house.

I said, "O.K."

He said, "You promise?"

I said, "Yeah, I promise. I'll come over tomorrow."

But I didn't. I broke my promise, that's what I did. I broke my promise.

—Landa

There was once this man who was a window cleaner in a town. His work was boring until he was washing a window in a school. He looked across the room seeing if any window was dirty. He saw this beautiful woman. She was the teacher at the school. He fell madly in love with her. His heart was popping out. He had to go and ask her for a date. After all the children left he asked. She knew she was engaged, but she said yes. So that night they went to a restaurant and ate. The man asked her to marry him, but she told him she was engaged. So when it was time to take the woman home, he said, "I'll never forget you."

The woman felt like crying, but she was engaged. The man walked sadly home and forgot about her.

—Lillian

The one or two girls in the group who had experienced sex wrote stories that were similar to those of their inexperienced

156

friends but that often ended in pregnancy and childbirth. The lovers in these stories also seem to live only for each other, in a way far distant from reality.

At the age of 11, Jane grew really lonely. But inside she knew of a secret love. (He didn't like her.) One night Jane dreamt that her and Patrick were in bed making love. It felt so good. Then Jane dreamt she was pregnant and was going to have a baby. She and Patrick ran away to the Bahamas, and Jane had the baby. They lived there forever.

—(Name withheld)

When I am lonely I turn on my radio. I feel like calling up Mike and telling him to get his ass over here. I feel like hitting the ball and running home. First base, second base, third base, home run.

When I'm lonely I hold Squeaky Pooh; he usually gets away. Then I transfer my thinking to Jonathan. I think about how cute he is and his adorable Jimmy Durante voice. He is the most adorable hunk of man. Boy would I like to be stuck on an island with him. Especially if we needed children to help us get off. He'd be a good provider. Then my thoughts transfer back to reality.

When I am lonely I pick up my cat, Pooh. I can do everything with him. I can curl him up into a ball. And I tell him my thoughts and problems. And how if my mother's mad I talk to my cat and say that I wonder how things would be if she never got mad at me. And sometimes I sit on the couch and listen to records and think about things. Sometimes I feel sorry for myself, and sometimes I don't.

What really gets to me is when I listen to that song "Mandy" on the radio. It's really a slow song, and it's sad. It makes me cry. Sometimes I think of the gorgeous tender lips on Mike. He's built so well. I can't wait.

—(name withheld)

The following piece concerns the painful discrepancy between fantasy and real life but also suggests that identification with a fictional character through reading or writing may bring a girl closer to her own experience.

I read this book last night and I interpreted myself as one of the characters, and it's been bugging me. The character's this girl, a senior in high school, and she's going out with this guy, Sean. She goes and gets herself pregnant and then at first, they were going to get married after they graduated, but then this guy went to his father and asked his advice, pretending it was his friend and his father said that he should drop the girl and not get married.

I could see myself one day being Liz, and it's been bugging me. I've been reading all these good romances, but it's just been killing me. Everything seems to work out so great in a book. They either get married or just something good happens.

—(name withheld)

Most of the girls were inexperienced in love-making, but this never stopped them from speculating. Remember kissing your pillow at night? Pretending it was *him*, instead of the goose down?

What a Kiss Feels Like

A kiss is kind of a mushy feeling, kind of like a vacuum cleaner pulling your lips against another's, a kiss is like floating on a cloud, and a kiss is also like you were dreaming.

—Laurie

A kiss feels terrific. It makes the heart pound faster. A kiss also is scary the first time. People kiss for hours on end. The air goes through their noses to keep their heart pounding faster.'

It was a warm summer day. The grass was very green. The daisies are all tilting to one side because of a slight wind. Their eyes meet. They run towards each other. Sally's thoughts are, Am I dreaming? Michael's thoughts are, Her lips are beautiful. What will they feel like against mine?

—Mary Ellen

A kiss makes you feel very close and personal. It makes your heart pump fast. You begin to see sky rockets. It's a great feeling. When your lips meet, so warm and tender, Lord, there's some

158

kind of sweet surrender.

Before the kiss: When the two lips are coming together, there's something in you that makes you feel loved and cared for by your lover.

—Mary Beth

When two people come together just about to kiss, they say to themselves, What's coming closer? I know what's coming closer, but it's just that I don't know what will happen next. I'm afraid to kiss. I never kissed before and all of a sudden they get so close that they kiss, and they then say to themselves, That wasn't so strange. It just felt like love.

—Faith

Romance group stories often ended with marriage. The girls wanted happy endings but in reality they viewed love as a terrific risk in which they could get hurt. When asked why marriage failed, they wrote, "The people involved do not understand each other," "One person annoys the other when they try to work," "quarrels over silly things." According to them, marriage brings out the Dr. Jekyll-Mr. Hyde in males, those demi-monsters who are sweet and seductive one minute, overwhelming the next. There was a widespread suspicion that regardless of his previous behavior and promises, a man after he is married may suddenly turn around and demand servility from his wife. They seemed to doubt their own ability to choose reliable mates and expressed the fear of being sexually used. They were afraid they would be unable to say no to a man.

As I was walking down the aisle in my long white gown with a big shocking pink bow on the back of it, I'm wondering what he is really like deep down inside. I've never been married before, and I am wondering whether I am going to be committed to wait on him hand and foot, or whether I'm going to be left alone and he is going to be very independent. I'm holding a bouquet of daisies and orchids. I have a bunch of people there dressed nicely and all standing there with big, bright, sunny smiles. The expression on my face is partly puzzled and very happy. My fiance looks like there is nothing on his mind. It doesn't look like he's puzzled or going to enjoy it or what. Well, we had a very nice wedding anyhow.

—Lisa

Men always like to get married, and so do some women. Here's a story about a marriage proposal.

My boyfriend, Roy, asked me to marry him, but I said, "No, I don't want to be married now. I'll get married when I feel like it."

He said, "But you feel like it."

And he kept asking me, and I kept saying no, no, no. He asked me again and started kissing all over me. Then he asked me again and I said, "Okay, Roy, Okay. Okay."

—Landa

The girls had varying opinions concerning the traditional roles of husbands and wives. Most wanted their husbands to share in the child care, but only a few expected help in house care. They all agreed that marriage ought to take place in one's thirties, and that having children, who are a time-consuming "commitment," would probably keep them from doing other things. Babies are not just cute, as they were for previous generations of young women; they are demanding, hard work. With very few exceptions, the girls said that they would not go to work during the first twelve years of their children's lives. They also planned on having interesting professional careers.

Perhaps they are more cautious about marriage than romance because they are thinking about their own mothers, most of whom work outside the home. The girls are as critical of their mothers as we were, but they are a little more specific in their criticisms: "She is overprotective," "She wants to keep everything clean," "My mom thinks she's ugly," "She jumps to conclusions," "She needs to lose fifteen pounds." Asked if they expected or wanted to be like their mothers when they grew up, only two of the twenty-five girls answered yes.

It is not unusual to receive the following kind of statement about marriage, children and careers:

> I'll stay single until I'm thirty because it is stupid to get married early. But I will get married. I feel I deserve a husband to make love to me so I can have kids. It's a possibility I'll get divorced. I will have children. I love kids. Kids, they're sweet when they are asleep.
>
> If I have kids, I wouldn't have a career because I have to take care of them like a good mother should. But I'd want a job. I want to be a doctor. I would do this afterwards.
>
> I would ask my husband to help me with the kids. I would do the housework, sweep, wash, cook, vacuum because that's not a man's place. If a man is single, he has to do the housework himself, but if a man's married, it's the woman who usually does the work.
>
> I believe in women's lib a little bit. It's a thing where women go to get their own rights against men.
>
> —Sabrina

There are frequent and heavy intrusions of reality in these stories; the writer's fears, self-doubts and conflicts are apt to be expressed, reflecting their actual lives and anxieties as well as their wishes. Romantic fantasy is born from emotional convictions that will govern many of our future actions. It reflects the quality of love one believes one deserves as well as the kind of lover one expects to be and to have: faithful, jealous, abusive, kind. The stories with which we entertain ourselves in girlhood stay with us and affect our choice of jobs, men, friends. Awareness of these fantasies may help a young woman to choose the direction of her life more consciously.

These writers seem more in touch with their romantic fantasies than were previous generations of women, as though the stories lived closer to the surface of their lives and were somehow easier to reach and a little less embarrassing to divulge. Would these fantasies have come out to the extent they did if there hadn't been a romance group? Certainly in the friendship groups some of them would have been expressed if not written; yet the sanctioned outlet during school hours may have lent credence and respectability to their feelings and made expressing them easier.

I was always impressed by the romance group's willingness to share their fantasies, however revealing. Members read their work to one another in a noncompetitive, mutually accepting environment. Although there was never ridicule on the part of the listeners, there was often self-conscious laughter on the part of the reader. The girls did not snitch or gossip, yet that possibility always existed. What were they getting out of these potentially embarrassing exposures? They were getting the knowledge and reassurance that other girls shared their fantasies. They seemed relieved that they were not so isolated, so peculiar, so *alone*. The writing and sharing of romantic fantasies eased their yearnings for boys they could not have, and softened the first painful stirrings of separateness.

Romance is a social ideal, a state of being in which nothing ever has to be worked out. There are no arguments over who does the dishes or who drives the car. It is a state toward which we all, subliminally, aspire in our relationships. Because we have all had a taste of it, in adolescence and at the beginnings of love affairs, we know it exists. Why do we want it? Perhaps if we lived our romances, we would never have to make compromises or adjustments in our relationships with our partners. The perfect mate would anticipate our every wish and would live to please us. Various temptations might slither in by way of rivals, money, power, but regardless of how many times lovers lost each other, there would always be happy endings.

The romance group, when asked the question "What is romantic?" came up with the following list:

1. A moonlight swim.

162

2. A picnic in the early morning.
3. A kiss.
4. A long walk along the beach in the dark.
5. A date.
6. A candlelight dinner.
7. A dark room.
8. When you're standing at the front door after a date with your boyfriend when he's about to kiss you goodnight.
9. Two lovers walking in a dark forest.
10. Sitting on the soft grass looking at the moonlight reflect on the pond.
11. A drive-in movie.
12. Whispering sweet nothings in her ear.
13. When they're right near kissing and a man throws his popcorn in front of them and they end up kissing the opposite sides of the popcorn box.

Perhaps some things never change. What makes moonlight so essential that no self-respecting romance can get along without it? The language of romance passes from one generation to the next as a kind of legacy. Each generation probably adds its own brand of realistic detail, but the same basic melodramas and motifs remain, from the first blush of attraction to the world melting away, leaving only the two lovers, self-contained on a starry, moonlit beach.

Recipes for Romance

Where and how do lovers meet? Ask the class to make a list of places and circumstances. (Introduction by friends, chance meetings, in a restaurant, at a dance, in a telephone booth, in a subway, at a friend's party, introduction through relatives, etc.) How do people feel when they first meet each other? Do they necessarily like each other right off? Write the thoughts of a person who meets someone but doesn't like him. Does her impression change or stay the same by the end of the first date or first evening together? What is a first impression? Write one. Remember, the main sensation in a first impression is newness, strangeness.

What is attraction? (Good for class discussion) Why are people attracted to each other? (Money, beauty or good looks, power, personality, humor, understanding, etc.) You might also try a class list with this question. What does a person have to have for *you* to be attracted to him?

What do lovers say to each other when they first meet? Write a dialogue of shy lovers, bold lovers, a shy lover and a bold lover.

You have a crush on someone who doesn't even know you're alive. Write the secret thoughts of a boy who has a crush on a girl. Now, write as a girl who has a crush on a boy. Are there differences between the two monologues? Do the differences reflect differences in feeling?

What is unrequited love? What does it feel like to love someone who doesn't love you back?

What are the blues? Have you ever had them? (The teacher might bring in a Billie Holliday blues album for the class to listen to.) What do the blues feel like? Write the lyrics for a blues song. The lyrics don't have to rhyme! They can tell a story of how your lover left you, or "done you wrong." If you have a blues melody in mind, you might be better able to write the lyrics. (The teacher might try playing a piece of music without words, as the students write. Just play it over and over. Turn out the lights, too. For contrast, she might bring in a current rock song that deals with the same feelings and problems, especially one that the students are listening to.)

Your date meets your parents. (How? Do you invite him over to dinner? Does he pick you up at your house?) What is their response to him? You might write a dialogue that includes the inner thoughts of one or both of your parents.

What would your parents say to you after you returned home from a date with someone they didn't like or approve of? What qualities or characteristics would they dislike in a date? Write a story in which they object to your date. Were they right? What is your opinion of the person? Your story, or dialogue, or statement, or monologue may be fictional or real, based on experience. It may also treat your parents' feelings about a friend, not necessarily of the opposite sex.

What is romance?

What is love?

What is romantic? Prepare a list. (Good for class project.) See "The Romantic Lives of Twelve-Year-Old Girls."

Are romance and love the same or different? Does one happen first? Can you have one without the other? What do people say when they are romantic? When they are in love?

You keep changing your mind. You are in love. You are out of love. You are in love. You are out of love. Write a poem (it does not have to, and probably should not, rhyme) or monologue in which you alternate rapidly between being in love and being out of love. You just can't decide. (You might talk about the other person's looks, character, actions, your own feelings about yourself and your vacillations, about life, love, anything that might come to a lover's mind as she falls in and out of love.)

What do people call each other when they are in love?

What is a romantic spot? A romantic setting? The most romantic spot and setting you can think of? What is an unromantic spot? Unromantic setting? The most unromantic? What makes a place romantic? What feelings does it inspire in people? Why do you think it has the power to do this?

Write a story describing a couple's first date. Their thirtieth date. Their last date. (Consider place, what people say to each other, how they treat each other, etc.)

Write a story about double-dating. Why do people double-date?

You look into his eyes. It's love at first sight! (Is there such a thing? Do you believe in it? Has it ever happened to you? To anyone, friend or relative, you know?) What does it feel like for both people?

Interview someone in your family or among your friends who has experienced love at first sight. Write or tape the interview. Share it with your class.

What does holding hands feel like?

What does a kiss feel like? (These two ideas may be developed by students with or without experience.)

A person asks another person to go steady. Write a dialogue.

A boy asks a girl to go to a dance with him. Write the dialogue. (Is the boy nervous? Confident? What about the girl? A nervous person would say different things, and behave differently, than would a confident person.)

Someone has just asked you to go steady, or to go out to a dance or dinner with him. How would you say no?

You are a rejected lover. He has just told you he doesn't love you, or doesn't want to go out with you, anymore. What did he say to you? How did it feel? What can you do to make yourself feel better? (Have a party? Eat an ice cream sundae? Call a friend? See a movie?) What can you say to yourself? Write a complaint about him: you must have been crazy, a fool, ever to have had anything to do with him.

Someone has just stolen your boyfriend from you. What are your feelings? Sour grapes? (You didn't really like him anyway.)

X loves Y, but Y doesn't love (might even hate) X. Write a dialogue between two people in which opposite feelings are expressed. Write another dialogue in which the feelings change.

X finds out that you are dating another boy. (How? Do you bump into him on the street? Does he come to your house and discover you with another person?) X is furious! Jealous! Try to explain what you were doing with Y. Does X believe you? What happens? (The idea is to try to explain seemingly inappropriate behavior.) What does Y say, if Y is there while you are explaining? What happens?

Write the monologue of a jealous lover.

X has betrayed you! X has disappointed you! (How? Late for a date? Out with another person? Doesn't call you on the phone for days or weeks? Tells a secret of yours?) How do you feel? Call him on the phone and tell him how you're feeling. What is his response?

X is two hours late for your date. Finally X shows up and says . . .

You gave X a piece of jewelry. You find out that X gave it away to someone else. (What was the piece of jewelry? Whom does X give it to? Why? Did you give X the piece of jewelry for a special reason?) Write X a letter. Then write X's reply.

If you had something difficult to say to your lover, would you say it face to face, on the phone or in a letter? What are hard things to say to another person? Why? (A proposal, you don't want to see this person any more, a complaint, a jealous accusation, an injured outcry, a criticism of your lover's behavior, a declaration of love.) Decide on something you or your character wishes to say to someone else she cares for. Write what she says face to face, then on the phone, then in a letter. Did what you say come out differently depending on the form of communication?

Write a love letter. You may also write the response to it. Why do people write love letters? (They may be far away from each other, embarrassed to say these things to each other face to face, see each other only once in a while, etc.)

You love each other, but you only see each other once a month. Why?

You started a pen pal relationship with a boy. You exchanged letters with him for a long time. The two of you lived far apart. Each sent pictures to the other and fell in love with the pictures. Then, after a long correspondence, you and he realized that you were in love. He now writes to tell you that he would like to visit you. You put off the visit. You make such excuses as "I've been sick." The truth is that you have (choose one, make up others): (1) sent him a picture of someone else; or (2) you put on or lost a great deal of weight, or lost your hair, or underwent a radical physical change. What do you do? What do you write? Does the person come to see you anyway? What happens?

What are the kinds of promises that lovers make to each other? (Prepare a list. This might be a good class project.)

How do lovers betray or disappoint each other? Make a list.

What qualities don't you like in a person?

X's former girlfriend is your jealous rival. She gets your boyfriend back. How? (What kinds of things do rivals do to get their man?) You might write this from the viewpoint of a rival.

Write a marriage proposal. (You might also set the scene; where does a marriage proposal take place in *your* imagination?)

How would you say no to a marriage proposal? How would you say yes?

X gives you, or you give *X*, an engagement ring. Write or describe the scene. It may take place in a jewelry store as the two of you pick out a ring. What does the ring look like? Do you agree? Disagree? Spend a long time trying to decide among rings?

Draw and describe a wedding dress, a dress that maids of honor might wear. Plan a wedding. Include everything you think ought to go into it. You may draw each thing or describe it. This may be a wedding you would like for yourself, or one you are planning for a friend.

Write a wedding ceremony.

What are you thinking about while you are walking down the aisle? (Male or female point of view, or both.)

Describe your feelings and thoughts before, during and after the wedding ceremony. You might think of this as a three-act play.

She doesn't show up at the wedding. What are the feelings and thoughts of the man who is jilted and the woman who jilts him? Why did this occur?

Before you get married, your mother tells you something important or gives you advice. What does she say?

How do you feel as you lean on your father's arm when you walk down the aisle?

Why do you think they call it "giving the bride away"? (Speculate on the history or mythology behind this expression.)

Do most people like weddings? Why? Have you ever been to a wedding? Describe it.

Interview your parents. What was their wedding like? Perhaps you can ask them to write a description of it with you. How did they feel before, during and after the ceremony?

What is a honeymoon? What is it for? Would you go on one? Where would you go? Write the dialogue of a newly married couple having dinner together on their honeymoon. What do they say to each other?

Lonely moments. What do you do when you're feeling lonely? When do you feel lonely? What do you think about? (Do you play records, read, lie on your bed, think, pet your cat, cry?)

What does it feel like to have a boyfriend or girlfriend? What are the good points and the bad of having someone?

At a marriage ceremony the person who officiates says, "If there is anyone present who knows a reason why this couple should not be wed, let him speak now or forever hold his peace." These words have just been spoken at your wedding. Suddenly from the back of the room someone shouts out. What does he say? What happens?

You run into a person on the street whom you once loved very much. What happens? Why did you part? What is the story of your past relationship? Can you tell this story from each person's point of view?

You had your chance, but you lost it. Now love is gone forever. Tell the story of this sad romance.

Write a lover's quarrel.

Write a lover's apology.

What does a person do to make someone like him? How does a person get the attention of the opposite sex? What do men do? Women? Do men and women act differently? How so?

X just isn't the one person for you. How do you tell her without hurting her?

What is your ideal boy like? When do you think about him most? What do you think about? Do you imagine your future with him?

What, or who, is your ideal girl? When do you think about her?

What do you think about before you go to sleep at night? Is this a lonely time for you? Do you ever think about the ideal boy or girl?

Make a list of self-criticisms.

Write a story entitled "An Impossible Love"; or "I Didn't Want to Leave"; or "I Should Never Have Done (or Said) It!"

A person whom you loved very much and whom you haven't seen for many years bumps into you on the street. You recognize her, but she does not recognize you. What do you do? What was your relationship like? What broke it up? What happens now?

You are going to faint, and your lover catches you before you fall. Just as you lose consciousness you see him. Describe this fully.

You are being pursued by three men who want to marry you. Each one has special qualities you like. You feel you must pick one. How are the three different? What is each man like? Why do you like each one? How does each one treat you? What does he bring out in you? Whom do you choose? Why?

A husband and wife are having a domestic quarrel. They do not agree about sharing household responsibilities. Describe their argument and the events leading up to it.

Should women work after marriage? After having babies? Would your wife?

Should a man do housework? Help with cooking? Clean up? Take care of the kids?

How are household responsibilities dealt with in your home?

Does romance stop after people are married? Why?

What does it mean to be "made for each other"?

How and why did your parents fall in love? Out of love?

How can you tell whether someone likes you? What are the signs? How do people show that they like each other? (Good for class project, as well as individual.)

You have been married for a while, but everything has not turned out as you wanted it to. You are now wondering whether you've made a terrible mistake. Describe your thoughts and feelings, or those of your character.

Complete these lines in any way you wish, with a lot of writing or a little:
   —My eyes met his and
   —His head came closer, then
   —My heart sank. I felt so hurt when she said
   —Her face changed and her warm hand gripped mine as
   —The blood started racing through me when
   —Rage burned within me and
   —Someday you'll wake up and find
   —I'll never forget how he
   —But it's all over now because
   —How was I to know that
   —She couldn't help
   —When I saw him for the first time I wanted to
   —I suppose you think I'm
   —Now that you know the truth I suppose you'll

A sailboat sinks in the Caribbean. A Navy captain and a fashion model escape on a five-foot raft. They survive for five days without water and with only some raw fish to eat. What are these two people like? (Change their professions if you want.) How do they treat each other? What do they talk about? Write a story about this romance.

Do opposites attract? Why?

The two of you are very different people. You have

almost nothing at all in common. Yet you fall in love. Write a story about such a couple. Does their relationship last? Why?

Anthology

Horror Stories

The Two Lives of Max Edgar

It was him and only him who alienated me from her eyes. She was my life, but that did not matter to him. He was cold, cruel. Oh, praytell, how could Carol fall in love with that Raven. I must kill him for my love for her is stronger than all of God's powers. But yet how? I cannot use a gun for I have no knowledge of how to use it. I know I will kill him with his inner fear, the fear of death. I had decided to do the deed October thirty-first, the day of the devil.

To think, all the love I had given her. How could she fall for him? Oh, I remember the first day I met her, at Sam Dillenger's party. She came in in her white ball gown, so beautiful. Trimmings of lace in a very mysterious color, very shimmering, as if it was the silk of God's rope. She was like her own goddess in her own way, in her *own* time.

I took her hand and asked if she would like to dance. My heart beat fast when I heard her so tranquil voice say, "Yes."

Those few hours we danced seemed like years, and those were golden years to me.

We had known each other for about a month now, and then he came along. Him. John Raven. His dark black hair always flashed in the sunlight, like a mirror in the full red sun.

I went to the pantry of my house. I gathered my best sheets and started cutting them into a robe and cloak. I must disguise my face, I thought. I went to the kitchen. I picked up a knife and cut myself, so that he would not recognize me. I cut right down my face. The blood disguised me. I was desperate.

I put on the hood and cloak and proceeded from the back door to his house, three blocks away. When I got there, I carefully, oh so carefully, opened the window. He was reading in his study. I crept up in front of him and said, "It's time to go."

He looked up in sheer fright. His face grew pale. And, as if he couldn't get the words out, he said, "Who are you?" He was never really a brave man, rather a coward, I say.

I said rather slowly, "I have come to get you. I am death." He grabbed his heart abruptly and then fainted dead away. Maybe it was because he had everything: money, no trouble, and my woman. At this thought my jealousy grew even more. Though he was dead, a heart attack seemed too good for him. I picked him up and started to strangle him with my bare hands and beat his head against the wall until blood trickled down the side of his neck. Then I dropped him to the floor.

Carol heard the noise and started yelling, "Help! Police!" I ran. I did not know whether she recognized me or not.

When I got back to my house, I took off the hood and cloak and burned them. I could practically see his face in the image of the flames. And then, I quickly got a towel from the pantry and wiped off the blood. The cut had started to heal by now and I thought it would be unnoticeable.

Then I heard a knock at the door. My heart beat fast. I

slowly went to open it. No one knew how relieved I was to find out it was only some children going Trick or Treat. After they had gone, I went to sit down and I heard another knock at the door. I was more relaxed and thought it to be more children, but I was wrong. It was the police. They arrested me and put me in jail.

The trial was the next day. Oh, how fast my heart beat when I stepped to the stand. They started to ask me questions. I answered as calmly as I could. Finally, I stepped down. Then Carol took the stand. I thought even if she had recognized me she surely would not tell on me, her love.

But then she started saying that she saw me kill him. No! No, this cannot be my Carol. It's an imposter. I jumped up and started to strangle her. It took four men to hold me back from her.

As they held me in my chair I couldn't tell what was going to happen. The jury whispered their answer to the Judge. And then those triumphant words: "We find Max Edgar guilty of murder and sentence him to the Black Castle."

A gasp filled the room, for he who entered the Black Castle did not come out.

The trip started on a dim afternoon. The sun shone like blood falling from the sky. The trip was to take three days, for the castle was in the middle of the desert. The days were blazing hot and the nights freezing cold.

At last we got. there. As I stood there, looking at the immense mixture of brick and pure terror, the gates slowly and quietly, as if in a cemetery, opened. The steel rusted gates. As I went in, I could see the moss and the slime dripping from the walls. I was taken below the ground to a dark brick cell, and then, as they pushed me in and locked and bolted the cell door, I could hear their footsteps echoing throughout the chamber halls.

I sat down, waiting for the unknown. Oh, how quiet it was! As quiet as silent death. I slowly laid my head on what was left of a rag pillow, then went to sleep.

Next morning, I was awakened to the sound of the opening of the chamber door. When I opened my eyes, on the floor lay a bowl of food, if it was food. I started to remember all the stories I'd read when I was young. One I remember called *The Count of Monte Cristo*. But I am not he, and I have no treasure waiting for me on the outskirts of the gates.

After several months passed, I felt I could stand it no longer. The pain, gnawing at my mind. I started to bang on the chamber doors, screaming until I thought my heart would burst. And then, while I still kept banging on the door, it came. The thing I had waited so long to see. It was the form of death I saw. I reached out as fast as I could to touch the hand of it. Then I felt myself risen. But then I dropped to the ground as I felt death slowly descending with me. For a second I thought, Does this mean I am going to hell? But then the Form of Death started to get wrinkled, the cloak seemed to be on fire. Before my very eyes, in a puff of smoke, it left me.

I got on my knees and prayed to death, What happened? Where death had been stood an angel. I asked it, "What happened? Why was the Form of Death deceased from my eyes?"

The angel slowly said, "The form you saw that you thought was Death was one of the Devil's servants. Now I am here to take you to our Holy King." Once again, I touched the hand of what I hoped was the real servant of God.

I felt myself being risen up past the ceiling, up past the clouds into Eternal Heaven, and I was set before the Holy God. He sat large upon the throne, a bold and masculine face with power almost bursting out of his hands. And then, in a voice as loud as thunder, he said, "Be you the poor soul, Max Edgar?"

I replied with a very slow yes. I thought to myself, Was this to be my second life? Up here in Heaven with God? Or was it to be in Hell with Satan?

God spoke the words, "Max Edgar, for doing a deed against my law, but yet being insane with jealousy, I set you forth on earth for one hundred years as a ghost."

The words stuck in my throat. Yet this still be a punishment? The thought alone, that in one hundred years Heaven still awaits me.

One of the angels led me out of Heaven, closing the gates behind me.

As I slowly lowered myself down to my former house, I saw another soul living there. It was *Carol*! I could see her, laughing with another man. Was this the same imposter who had sent me to the Black Castle? Or had my real Carol turned against me? I came closer to hear what they were saying.

He was saying, "Carol, did you honestly love that murderer, Max Edgar?"

And then the word I wished I had never heard. "No," she replied.

That word. I forbid my ears to hear it. If Carol could not love me, she would not love anybody. I slowly approached her. But I felt a hand holding me back.

It was John Raven! He said, "Max, it is not worth killing another, although I would have liked to when I found out she didn't love me either."

For the first time, I started thinking of him as a human. We slowly started walking up the garden. For the first time, we started talking as friends, not enemies. The next day we started looking at all the changes made. Someone named Ford made a very different way of travel. It did not run on horses. It ran on en-gine, I think it was called.

As the many years passed, John Raven stayed with me for my one hundred year sentence. God did not object to this for it was better that the one I had killed had become my eternal friend than my eternal enemy. After a long time of waiting, after seeing Carol take men and then leave them I went back to Heaven and to the Holy God.

With his thundering voice, he said, "Now that you have

finished your hundred year sentence and John Raven has forgiven you for your deed, I set you forth, here on Heaven."

To my surprise I saw the ghost of Carol walking up to God. God said, "Carol Charles, for causing men's insanity and causing the death of John Raven and Max Edgar, I forthwith sentence you to the Land of Satan."

Her head nodded in sorrow. She looked to me. "Max, tell him it isn't true."

But what she had done to me she could never repair. With a solemn look, I said, "No." I saw her lowered down to the underworld.

I set out to explore what the Holy Land was.

Heaven was a mass of mist that could be shaped in any form that pleased you. My main enjoyment was the wall of heaven that stretched across the sky. All its doors of gold were filled with enjoyment for all. But for one door. It was dark and grim. Upon a day of sun and light Max Edgar asked one of the angels about the old door.

He said, "That's where death really begins."

Max Edgar did not understand this, but on July 1, 1907, Max Edgar entered the door and never came out.

—Nicolas Bunin

I found myself pushing, forcing my way through skeletons for what—I hadn't the slightest. Suddenly I was falling, trying to reach something to grab. It was there, but it wasn't. Suddenly I was drowning. I see a skeleton reaching for me. Now it's death reaching. I'm being pulled into darkness, falling drowning death.

—Danny Goodwin

The Thumb

How can one live with a thumb which is terrifying to mankind? I'll tell you this story which will give a chill to your spine.

My, how old a woman can be without age. Rain fell upon her head. With tiredness she walked trying to find some shelter. The houses passed her like forgetness leaving her alone in the world.

I'm not going into that house she said, when she passed the house of death. Old Mr. Greenwich lived there. No one knew how he could live in a house so dark to the eye.

No shelter left to go to, only that forbidden place. She walked toward it with life walking away from her. She knocked twice . . . twice and at last she heard someone.

"Come in," said the dark shaped figure. "I saw you by the house lots of times, I was wondering why you didn't come in." She stared at his left hand. Why didn't he have a thumb, where had it gone?

She walked through the dark halls. Suddenly he turned around and his thumb grew from its knuckles and she saw him nearer until he had killed her with a shocked experience.

—Josephine Tavera

Head

Imagine a chopped head with an axe in it, image all the blood falling out. Image your brain being chopped in half and you wouldn't be able to think with all your wasted knowledge and all your brains sticking out with blood?!?! And a bloodie axe on your mind and every time you tried to think your mind would bleed.

—Dorrie Jones

My Imaginaree Enemy

Mr. Hands is a pair of hands who always tried to pull me and cut my legs up. I never saw it because it was always dark. Boy was I scared. But I felt safe under the covers. Also I looked at the wall I got scared. My mother said it was my imagination. She was right.

—Bernadette Fife

All over there were men women and kids hanging by their necks with blood rolling down their bodies their insides sliding out their eyes had been poked out with red hot copper coins under them on the floor were pieces of their morsels with rats feasting on them a three year old had been flogged everbody was crying or dead their stomachs were ripped open half digested food with bloody morsels hung out. Boo.

—Frank Whelan

One night I was listening to Sherlock Holmes on WRVR radio. A snake was put into a woman's bedroom and it strangled her. Ever since then I have had a fear of snakes strangling me while I'm sleeping.

I was in bed in the house my mom and dad rented in Long Island. There were plenty of houses around but we didn't know anybody that lived in them. My sister was in N.Y. at my grandmother's. My mom and dad were asleep in their bedroom. I know because I heard them snoring. It must have been around 1:30 am. I was lying awake. I heard a bump near the window. I jumped. I heard another one opposite, near the closet. My heart started beating very fast. Very fast! I kept hearing them in different parts of the room. I thought it might be a snake. I decided to call my mother: "Mom . . . mom . . . mommy . . ." "What is it Nicole?" "I keep hearing bumps in my room and I'm scared." "Don't worry. It's probably just your imagination." "Mom, couldn't you just come sit with me till I go back to sleep?" "Alright." So she came into my room and sat with me. After around ten minutes she left, thinking I was asleep. (The bumps stopped while she was in my room, which was really maddening because that *really* made her think it was my imagination.) The bumping started again, I was getting more and more terrified. I really began to think it was a snake. I am very scared of snakes. After a long time I went back to sleep. I was probably too scared to stay awake. I never found out what caused the bumping.

—Nicole King

Love At First Sight

A girl was riding on the bus one day. Her name was Brenda Polic. A man grinned at her. She started a conversation. They talked and talked. Finally her stop came. She said, "I have to get off, but why don't you come to my house at 7:00 for dinner and we'll talk more?"

So he came at 7:00. They talked and they fell in love. They got married a week later.

One month later, the husband came home from work one day. He yelled, "Honey, I'm home."

Nobody was there, and there was no supper. She came back one hour later. She was pregnant.

He screamed, "Where were you?" He took her by the neck, not realizing she was going to have a baby, and slammed her head against the wall five times, and then kept on choking her. Finally he saw she was going to get a baby and let her go, but it was too late. He had already murdered

186

her, but he started to see the baby come out. He called the hospital.

They took the baby out, and the baby went up for adoption because the mother died and the man ran away. They kept the baby in the hospital for one year because she was too small to go up for adoption. After one year the baby had died because it didn't have the proper love with a mother and father.

This is how it happened. The baby was crying one day for three hours and nobody stopped her from crying. Finally she cried so much she lost her breath and died. The baby was very weak because the father used to drink and smoke mariwana and the mother didn't have the baby right because the mother died and the baby came out.

So as the world went on the accidents and mystery cases went on. You think back to all those mysteries. You remember all of them and watch out for them.

Adventure Story

"Hey, Hilary, listen, there's a bunch of natives on that island we blew an atom bomb on. We think they're still alive but they might be awfully shook up. Go in the *Skimmer* and help them to the hospital. Okay?"

"Roger," I said, and went to gather up my first aid kit. "Damn that bomb! Making so much trouble for some people who wouldn't harm a—a flea!" I was pretty shook up myself!

"They're cannibals!" announced Sharon, my 12-year-old daughter. I turned around angrily. "Would you like to come with me and see just what kind of people they are?" I asked. She agreed and we set off 5 minutes later in our houseboat, *The Skimmer I.*

"There they are! I see them!" Sharon called to me. "They're all standing there as—as if they, um, expected us!"

"Who are?"

"The can—uh, the natives!"

I smiled with the knowledge that I had proved my point.

I pulled up along the beach, and drew in my breath as I stepped on land. Behind me, I heard Sharon gasp and when I turned around I saw she had run back to the boat.

I only wished I could have.

They stood like zombies, blood painted on their flesh, their arms hanging lifelessly at their sides, their eyes staring lifelessly at the open sea. I realized that they wouldn't come with me, that they were waiting for their God to come himself. . . .

"Come!" I called. The waves broke on the sunny beach, the birds sang, Sharon sobbed on the boat, and the natives didn't move, but stood with their eyes fixed rigidly on the sea. . . .

I took the hand of the nearest one. "Come on!" I tried again. Sharon screamed, and I found myself holding a torn piece of skin in my hand while the native had collapsed at my feet. . . .

I turned and ran to the boat. "Damn atoms, damn bombs, damn wars," I muttered and pulled out, while they still stood with their eyes fixed rigidly on the sea. . . .

—Yvonne S. Kingon

Mystery Stories

The Wilson Murders

Chapter I: The Lime Pit

In a lime pit that smelled sour a woman was dead. She was lying face down with her hands stretched out over her head and her feet were stretched. She was all mushy, decaying rapidly. Her skin was dissolving, burning off. She was a horrible scene. She didn't have a face anymore. All the garbage and debris was scattered around her. She had a death grip on the ground. Her fingernails were long.

It was about 6 A.M. in the morning. Dew was just coming up. The light was just beginning to hit earth. A dog, a fox terrier, ran through the farm door out into the fresh morning air. He went to the lime pit where he always used to go to smell the lime. The dog started barking, like the cry of a whimpering baby.

Joe, Marty and his farmhand, Terry, came running. They

189

were surprised the dog was barking because he did not bark much.

"If we don't catch that dog, he'll run into the neighbor's field and start eating the corn!" Suddenly Joe, Marty and Terry stopped three or four feet from the lime pit.

"Do you smell what I smell?"

"What do you smell?"

Joe looked a little frightened. He knew that his sister Suzanna had been missing for the last four days. Joe and Marty suddenly glanced into the pit and saw a few bones, a few chips of teeth and some brunette hair.

They were sure it was Suzanna.

Chapter II: The Lab

The police stood a few feet from the lime pit. "Have the remains out and we'll identify it at the lab."

They wore masks in order to go down the lime pit to keep smell away. They searched the area for clues. They went down in the pit with a hoist and carriage.

The policeman who was searching for clues came back with no clues.

At the lab they found an imprint of a horseshoe on the skull. They identified the bones to be whatever was left of Suzanna Wilson.

"Sergeant, come over here," said the puzzled police scientist. "We've found a horseshoe imprint on the remains of this lady's head."

"I think you're right." The sergeant asked the scientist, "What do you think happened?"

"It seems as if it was somebody hit her with the horseshoe because the wound didn't go too deep in. If it were a horse the wound would be in bigger and deeper."

"The murderer could have had the horseshoe on his fist and hit her on the head."

"But there was no evidence of a horseshoe in the pit."

"We could take an autopsy to find out if it was a horse or a man."

"She could have been killed by someone playing horseshoes and who probably didn't want her around and hit her on the head by accident. When he found out that she was dead, he picked her up and put her in the lime pit."

"Can you round off the day she was killed?"

"April 21st."

Chapter III: Zachary Smith

Detective Zachary Smith was short, had blondish hair, wore a Sherlock Holmes hat, and was very intelligent in his way of finding things out. He was the famous Z. Smith who had found who murdered Benjamin Franklin, a famous toothpaste man. He had also solved a lot of other murder mysteries in New York.

He lived with his mother down in the country. His father had died in 1972. So all he had was his mother to talk to. She was an elderly woman, kind at heart, and a gourmet chef, yet she wasn't a very good entertainer. She mothered Zachary a lot. She let him have his way most of the time. She gave him privileges, a lot of them. He had had a detective set when he was a kid. He was very good at school, paid attention and did what he was told. At home he also did what he was told, and if he didn't his mother would ask him again, sharply.

He had always known life ever since he ran away. He robbed a food store for he was so hungry and was put in the slam. After one month in the cage he never left home again.

He was a private eye. His office was in order, no papers hanging around, no newspapers or books all over the place. He kept his information in order, and his file cabinets were in a way old, so they were hard to open. He had a lot of books on detectives. He had a green pad on the desk, a turning chair, five drawers, and a lamp that was black on the bottom, a white button and a cord going up to the light. If he knew that a man committed a crime, he would shine the light in the man's, or woman's, eyes, and he used a tape recorder to record what he or she said. He is a very famous detective. He had a guard outside his door because other people wanted to get him back.

Joe Wilson was not a neat country boy with a checkered shirt. He was pretty chubby, and, as much as he worked on the farm, he was lazy and liked to eat.

Joe was walking into the detective's office, sweaty from jogging over from the farm.

"Mr. Smith, I'd like to get this case over with because I'd like to find out who killed my sister. When I get my hands on him, there ain't gonna be no more of him." He was standing up, and he had his hands covering his face. He squatted down and was crying.

"There's no sense of crying. It's already happened. What's happened, my dear man?"

"My sister, Suzanna Wilson, died in a lime pit on the day of April 21st. She said she was going for a walk with our dog to the bridle path where our horses go. Then I heard a scream, but I thought it was just one of the kids fooling around. The dog came back, but not Suzanna. We thought she might have just gone for a longer walk. I thought she just might have gone somewhere for a while. It's happened before. She hasn't called or notified us for days. I hadn't known what happened during those periods."

"Have you notified the police?"

"Yes, but they haven't done anything about it."

"The fee will be fifty dollars."

"I'll pay anything just to get the murderer of my sister."

"Joe," said the detective. "We'd better go to the bridle path to look for anything suspicious."

Chapter IV: At the Bridle Path

Mr. Smith, the detective, and Joe Wilson, the brother of Suzanna, drove down to the bridle path. While they were riding on the bridle path, they found a piece of Suzanna's jewelry. It was a squash blossom necklace.

"That's Suzanna's! She must've been here!"

"Looks like there was a struggle." They had found scuffled footprints and a drag mark. The ground was very soggy.

"Aha!" said Zachary Smith. They looked into the corner where the bridle path turned and they saw the imprint of a lady's body.

"That's Suzanna's!" In a sad voice he started to cry.

"How do you know?"

"I can tell because that's her shoe over there." A black leather boot that was ripped. It had three drops of blood on it and it had no heel.

Zachary picked it up, put it in a bag with the jewelry, got on his horse, and rode back to the car.

After they got back to the detective's office, they gave the jewelry and the boot to the Fingerprint Office. "Put it under the microscope to see whose fingerprints it is."

Then the phone rang. Zachary Smith answered it. It was a very low, mysterious voice.

"If you keep looking for the murderer of that girl, Suzanna Wilson, I'll kill you just like *someone* killed her."

"Who is this anyway?"

"This is *Someone*."

The detective heard a click, then a dial tone. Mr. Smith set a guard outside his office.

"Joe, I think that phone call was just a big clue. Someone called and said that he was going to kill me just like Suzanna. Then I asked who it was."

"And what did he say?"

"He said it was 'Someone'."

Joe shook his head.

"You go back home. If I get any information, I'll call you."

Chapter V: The Operator

Zachary had just arrived at the Bell System Telephone Company. He showed his badge.

"Can I please have the number that just called 346-2222, my number?"

The operator stuttered, "Ah-ah-yeah-yeah. The number that just called your office is 226-2444."

"I wonder whose number that is?"

"It's the Wilson's. Did you know their sister has been missing for a long, long time? About three days."

"Oh, really? Did you know Suzanna?"

"Yeah, very well."

"What is she like?"

"She is kind of a tomboy. We were friends in high school. Everyone says she's cheap. She always wears tons of make up, but looks very pretty with it on. She's very kindhearted. We're still friends."

"Oh? What do you mean by that? Can you give me some examples?"

"Why are you asking all these questions, anyway?"

"You might as well know the truth. But promise not to tell anyone. I'm a detective. Suzanna Wilson is dead."

"No! No, she can't be!"

"Well, she is."

"How did she die?"

"She was found in a lime pit, dissolving."

"Poor girl. Who murdered her?"

"We don't know yet. Are you sure that call came from the Wilson residence?"

"Sure."

He thought to himself, I better stake out the Wilson's.

"Did Suzanna have any friends?"

"Yes, Joshua Zoolosky was her boyfriend. He was jealous, selfish, not kind. He liked animals and whenever he was mad at the world he turned to animals. He worked as a veterinarian, and he had a special way with animals. He could almost talk to them. But to his girlfriend he was always cruel. Everytime she did something wrong to him, he would always smack her in the face. When she was in the mood to say she was sorry, he wasn't. He was grouchy all the time."

"Why did she love him?"

"She was drawn to him because of his unusual talent of understanding animals. And because she was lonely. And because he was handsome."

"Where did she live?"

"201 Elmstreet. It's a cottage a little way off from the farm house."

"Thank you. You've been a great help."

Chapter VI: A Visit to the Victim's House

"This must be the place," said Zachary. He wore a gray suit, a tie, his hair was combed down, patted on the side, with a lot of hair spray. He carried a black attache case like it was a part of his body. In it were papers of great importance to his cases.

Suzanna's cottage looked dirty and dusty. Shutters that need repair, sagged. The front door looked as if it had been partly open, as if it had been pried.

"Hello? Is there anybody there?" He was in the living room. The drapes were torn. The couch was messed up and tipped over. A drawer that was in the coffee table was open, and there were papers scattered all around it. He bent down, picked up the papers, folded them, and put them in his pocket. Zachary felt that the living room, despite having been rummaged through, gave the impression that Suzanna Wilson lived a sheltered life. On the exterior she pretended to be

195

different. The room was painted in a dense green, imprints on the rug showed that the furniture was never really moved from its place. She didn't really look for anything new, she kept her house the way a person who was grieving over some forgotten incident would.

He walked into the study and found a photo in it of Suzanna and a man. At the bottom of the photo it said "Love, Joshua."

"So that's Joshua!"

Now he glanced over to the desk. Strangely enough only one drawer was open and had been rummaged through. He examined the contents and he found a booklet. As he looked at each page he finally deducted that it was a diary that Suzanna had been writing. The diary stopped on April 20th, a day before Suzanna was killed. After April 20th some pages had been ripped out. He wondered where the pages could be and if anyone had taken them.

Suddenly Zachary heard a noise at the door. The door was halfway open. Marty Wilson, Suzanna's younger brother, was standing there.

"What are you doing here?"

"Looking for clues."

"What kind of clues?"

"Any kind of clues."

"Oh."

Zachary picked up the diary and showed it to Marty. He opened the book and turned to the pages that had been torn out.

"Do you know who tore these pages out?"

"No. Probably Suzanna." Marty looked very nervous and tense. Zachary Smith thought it was because he was thinking about his sister Suzanna.

"Why would she want to tear something out of her own diary?"

"I don't know." Marty turned around quickly. "Well, I better go now." Marty left.

196

Zachary thought Marty was a bit suspicious.

Chapter VII: Mama's Boy at Dinner

"Hello, Mother, is dinner ready?"

She took off her apron and got ready for dinner. "I have to freshen up a little." All her make up wore off in the cooking steam. She felt that she looked simply awful and half dead without make up on.

This was the menu: first course, French onion soup and snails under glass; second course, chow mein with fried rice and French bread; and for dessert, Angel Food cake with chocolate icing saying "To My Dearest Son, Zachary" in white icing, and an angel wearing a banner saying "To the Best Detective of Them All."

Then, after dinner he laid down on the couch and turned on the television to the news, listened to it for about half an hour.

"Mama! I have to go now."

"Wait. Can't you wait a little longer?"

"Just a little longer."

"Help me with the dishes."

"Okay, just hold on."

While they were washing the dishes, the phone rang. It was Joe.

"Zachary?"

"Yeah?"

"I've got another suspect for you. My younger brother, Marty."

"I'll be right over."

They hung up.

"Mom, I've got to go now."

Chapter VIII: Surveillance on the Wilson Farm

Outside on the Wilson's farm, it was pitch black. The owls were hooting, the cows were asleep. It was a dark, gloomy night. The ground felt like he was walking on a bed. Suddenly, something fell on his back. It practically scared the daylights out of him. Zachary whipped out his .38 and turned around and said, "Freeze!" It was only an old rotted branch that fell off an old oak tree. He asked himself, Was it sawed off on purpose, or did it just fall off?

He started walking towards the house. He walked up the steps. They were creaking. When he came to the front door, he found that the house was pitch black. All the rooms were dark, except one, the living room. You could hear the clock ticking for miles. He saw Suzanna's picture on the living room side table. She had dark black hair, blue eyes, and she looked younger than when they found her dead. She was pretty.

Just then Zachary Smith heard footsteps coming down the stairs. Joe walked into the living room.

Zachary Smith came out of his hiding place, behind the couch. He walked up to Joe. "Did you make a phone call from the house recently?"

"Well, that doesn't really matter. What I have to tell you is more important. I have some information on who might have killed Suzanna. Matter of fact, I am sure who did it—" Suddenly Joe dropped to the floor and Zachary Smith saw him with a knife in his back. Zachary bent down to examine the body. He pulled out the knife with his gloves on and wrapped it in a towel.

"The man who murdered Joe must have murdered Suzanna!" He said, "Well, that drops Joe as a suspect."

He went out the door and got in his car and drove away to his office. Then he called the police.

Chapter IX: Joshua Zoolosky

Joshua Zoolosky worked at the Noah's Ark Animal Hospital, 1212 Muleberry Street. He owned the block because he was an animal doctor and he got a lot of money. Zachary Smith was in the hospital and couldn't find him in his office. He got back into his car and decided to drink a Scotch. When he went to a nearby bar he saw Joshua Zoolosky.

Joshua was tall and had dark brown hair, a long beard, blue eyes, and a lot of freckles, and a mustache. He was playing darts.

Zachary Smith came up to him. "Joshua Zoolosky, I presume?"

"Yes, I'm me, alright." He was really drunk. "And don't tell me—you're *you*!"

"You're absolutely right. I am Zachary Smith. I would like to ask you a few questions. I'm a private detective."

"No, sir! I'm playing darts with Shorty."

"Where were you approximately fifteen minutes ago?"

"Where were *you* fifteen minutes ago?"

"Suzanna Wilson was killed in the last 72 hours and her brother Joe was just discovered murdered about an hour ago. You are a suspect."

"No! It ain't me. I didn't kill Joe because I've been here all night playing darts. I have witnesses to prove it."

"Like who?"

"Like Shorty. And Smitty." One was about 7'9", he could have been Wilt Chamberlain's twin. The other was about 4'1", bald, and had a patch over his eye.

"Do you drink like this often?" Zachary asked.

"Not 'til Suzanna died."

"Where were you the day Suzanna died?"

"I don't know. I don't know when she died."

"It was in the newspaper. It was April 21st, in case you haven't looked."

"I was in my office with my animals."

"Did anyone see you?"

"My nurse saw me when I checked out."

"Was she there when you checked in?"

"No."

"How about tonight when Joe was killed?"

"I've been right here in the bar, drinking with my friends, Shorty and Smitty."

"Did you have a relationship with Joe?"

"I knew him. I was his veterinarian. He brought animals to my hospital and I went to the farm sometimes."

"Did you ever go to Suzanna's cottage on the farm?"

"Yes, once."

"What did you do there?"

"I just stayed with her."

"Have you ever read what she wrote in her diary?"

"No!" He was very mad. "And stop asking me questions!"

"Did you fight with Suzanna often?"

Pow! Joshua punched Zachary right in the nose. It was bleeding. It was broken. It felt sore and all broken up, like the bone had gone right up to the brain.

Zachary Smith got up, brushed off his pants and walked out.

Chapter X: Mama's Boy at Breakfast

In the morning Detective Zachary Smith woke up with a really sore nose and thought to himself, That was a brave thing for me to do. He walked downstairs and said, "Ma-ma! What's for breakfast?"

"What happened to your nose! Where were you last night? Oh! Let me get you a bag of ice. Does it hurt?"

"Yeah, it hurts, what do you think—it tickles?!" he said in a grouchy voice.

"Oh! Let me give you a nourishing breakfast and then I'll

200

take you to the doctor's." She laid him down on the couch and turned on the television and went into the kitchen to start cooking.

"The bacon is in the oven. Tell me what happened last night."

"Well, you know I'm on that case about Suzanna Wilson. I went to talk with her boyfriend at the bar and I started asking him questions. I think he got a bit frustrated. Then he gave me the old one-two-three in the nose."

"Oh, Zachary! Don't you know that I don't like you going to bars?"

"Ma! I'm 29! Anyway, stop bugging me. It was nothing."

A big bruise covered the whole nose and part of the eyes. It was a very pale white and had a really deep black and a medium blue.

They smelled a really weird smell. Mama jumped up and said, "My bacon!" She went to the stove. It wasn't burnt, it was just right.

Fifteen minutes later his mom called him in and said, "Breakfast time!" He looked on the table and there was toast, coffee, milk, orange juice, eggs, pancakes, and bacon.

"I can't eat all this!"

"I'll help you. Start eating."

They finished breakfast. "I'm going over to Suzanna's other brother's, Marty."

"But be careful."

He ran out of the house and got into the car before his mother remembered that she wanted to take him to the doctor.

Chapter XI: The Dog

Zachary drove down to the farm in his Hornet Sport-About. The car ride was bumpy and whenever it started it always backfired. It was getting bumpy because the roads

201

down to the Wilson farm were just dirt roads and the pebbles made it hard to drive. He thought to himself that he would go down to the farm and try to find some things that might have been used in the murders. He was most specifically looking for the gun the Wilsons' parents had been killed with seventeen years ago and the horseshoe that Suzanna was killed with.

He expected to find Marty at the farm. He was thinking to himself that Marty could have been the murderer.

Zachary pulled up into the driveway. His car skidded lightly. He went in the house. The house was very dusty. The paint was chipped. He felt very uneasy. He turned at the slightest movement. A rat appeared. "Something's going to happen to me," he murmured. His heart was thumping so hard that he felt like leaving.

He was wondering why Terry wasn't there. He had expected Terry to be at the farm. He decided to go into Joe's room. He looked around to make sure that no one was in the room. He looked up at the wall and saw a picture of Suzanna taped to a dart board. There were dart holes all over her face. It gave him the chills. He moved back to get a better look. He stood still, frozen in astonishment.

Suddenly he heard small taps and scratching coming from the stairs. He got real scared. He felt like it was going to be the end of his life. His heart started beating a little too fast, like a horse gallop. He drew his gun and ran out of the room to the head of the stairs, only to find a dog, a fox terrier mutt. He laughed to himself and put his guns away.

Zachary could see the dog's ribs through his skin. The dog was crawling up the stairs, crying; he could hardly make it. He picked up the dog, "Poor thing, you look hungry," and he slowly walked down the stairs making sure he wouldn't trip.

He recognized the dog as the one who found Suzanna's body. He put the dog in the front seat of his car and drove home as fast as he could without going over the speed limit.

Chapter XII: The Horseshoe

When Zachary got the dog home he fed the dog ground beef with pieces of cheese in it. The dog ate it as fast as he could and then cried for more. Zachary said, "Hmm, you are hungry, aren't you?"

The dog laid his body down next to Zachary's feet and then he rolled over like he wanted to be scratched on his belly. Zachary scratched him on the belly for about an hour. He didn't want to scratch him anymore because his arm was aching him so, but he didn't want to leave. The dog finally got up and walked off to a cozy place on the couch and fell asleep.

Zachary went off to take a nap, also, but when he got up and returned to the living room the dog wasn't there. The window had been left open. He looked out the window and saw footprints on the muddy ground. He tried to follow the footprints, but they stopped at the concrete sidewalk. Zachary felt sad because he had found this dog and really liked it. He felt guilty because he had left the window open. He was worried that the dog might starve or could get run over by a car. He remembered when he picked up the dog and put him in his car. The dog had looked at him, hungry and scared and sad.

By now it was dark, so Zachary went to bed. He dreamed about the way the dog looked in the car. He dreamed about the dog again and again and again. Suddenly, he felt a thump on his chest. It knocked the wind out of his sails. He turned on the bed table light and he saw the dog, with its paws on his chest. The first thing he was going to do was to get up and feed the dog. He sat up in bed. He felt something fall off his chest into his lap. He looked down and saw a horseshoe that had dried blood on it. He rushed it right down to the lab. It turned out to be Suzanna's blood on the horseshoe.

Chapter XIII: The Fingerprints

The lab was all white with all these special medical instruments. There were three doctors looking at other fingerprints and cases. Zachary Smith walked in and handed them the horseshoe with a gloved hand. One of the doctors immediately took it and then took the Suzanna Wilson murder case out from the files. There were many people who were suspects: Joshua Zoolosky, Joe Wilson, his brother Marty, and Terry the farmhand. The doctor tried to find out whose fingerprints matched the ones on the horseshoe. The doctor looked at Zachary Smith with a confused look and said, "The fingerprints on the horseshoe match the ones of Joe Wilson."

"Oh, my God," said Zachary, and he thought to himself, But who could have murdered Joe?

He went to his office, which was in the same building as the lab. He went into his safe and took out a paper bag. He walked fast back to the lab. Once he got there he took a look at Suzanna Wilson's file and then handed the bag to the doctor.

"Doc, whose fingerprints are on this knife?" He opened up the paper bag and pulled out the knife that had killed Joe. Zachary had pulled it out of Joe the night Joe was murdered and he had kept it in his safe, hoping that the murderer might come to him searching for the incriminating knife.

The doctor had been working at least five minutes now, and finally found out who killed Joe. He turned to Zachary and looked more confused than ever. "It was Marty Wilson, Joe Wilson's younger brother."

"It's kind of weird, but everyone in that family is killing each other."

Chapter XIV: At Joshua's House

Zachary went to Joshua's house because he wanted to check out his suspects and because he wanted to find some clues. Zachary rang the doorbell and Joshua answered the door with a mean grin on his face.

"Hi, inspector, what did you want?" He had a cat in his hand and he looked down at it and said, "Why did he have to come and ruin my day?"

The cat jumped out of Joshua's hand and ran into the bedroom. "Come in, inspector, or may I call you Zachary?"

Zachary sat down on the over stuffed couch. He looked around the room and saw a few dogs, a canary, and posters and stickers from the A.S.P.C.A. posted all over the place. He felt very uncomfortable with all the animals and ten million eyes looking at him. There was a musty fragrance in the air.

"You want a drink?"

"Yeah, Scotch."

Joshua left the room and walked into the kitchen to get a drink. He thought, Why the heck is he here? Joshua looked out of the kitchen and saw Zachary looking through the drawers of his desk.

"This is it," Zachary said, as he pulled some pages out of the desk. He stuck them in his coat pocket.

Joshua walked into the living room with the drinks in his hands. Zachary took the pages out of his pocket. He had a very strong look on his face.

Joshua looked stunned.

Zachary shoved the pages in Joshua's face. "What are you doing with this and where did you get it?"

They both sat down. Joshua buried his face in his hands, his elbows sank to his knees. He said, in a sobbing voice, "Someone sent it to me anonymously in the mail."

"Why did you keep it?"

"Because I wanted something to remember Suzanna by. I was scared to tell the police."

Zachary read the pages.

Chapter XV: The Diary

"April 21st: I still remember so well the night my parents were killed. It was 8:30 at night and the whole family, except for Joe who was out with friends, was watching T.V. Joe was out at a beach party. As we were watching T.V. we heard some creaking sounds, as though someone was walking around the house. Then someone in a black mask and black pants and a black suit came bursting through the door, shouting, 'Don't move!'

"Just then my mother and father got up to bring me over to where they were sitting. I was eight years old. Then, before my mother or father could hide for shelter Bang! went the pistol two times. And then my Mom and Dad were dead. I screamed as loud as I could, then quietly shut up, scared that he would shoot me. But then he got really bloodshot eyes and seemed to be crying—I could see his eyes through his mask. Then he ran out. I didn't hear a motor, so I suspect he either walked or bicycled away.

"My Dad was face down on the floor. My Mom was laying face up on the couch. There was blood oozing out of her. And when I went an inch closer I could see her guts. It was grossifying.

"I was crying with all my might. Marty was a baby and still asleep, having no idea of what was going on. I knew who the murderer was right from the start. It was Joe. I could tell by his eyes.

"When he came back to the house, I was still crying. He acted really upset. He had a big beach jacket on. One of his pockets was really bulging with something. He leaned down to put his jacket over my mother and a black mask fell out of his pocket.

"After this, whenever Joe asked me to do something, I

always did it! I was scared half to death to make him angry. I knew if he got angry I'd get killed, too.

"I lived with him in the farmhouse until I was 17, when I moved into the cottage an acre away from the farmhouse. I am writing this so that if I die someone will find this and know who killed my parents. I am very frightened of Joe, and I'm never going to say anything about it unless someone finds this.

Suzanna Wilson

Zachary looked up at Joshua and said, "She must have really been scared of him."

"Yes," Joshua said, "I tried to ask her to come live with me and marry me, but he wouldn't let her. I usually don't drink, but this whole thing has had me so cooped up that I've had nothing else to do."

Just then, Joshua's little kitten jumped up in his lap and started rubbing against his stomach.

Zachary asked, "How did Suzanna and Marty get along?"

"She was scared of him, too. Just because he was a man. She was also very scared of me sometimes."

"Marty still working on the farm?"

"I'm not sure, but I think so, why?"

"Because Marty killed Joe and I'm trying to find him."

"You'd better watch out—Marty's very slick."

Chapter XVI: Terry the Farmhand

Zachary Smith went back to the Wilson farm, looking for clues as to where Marty was. He saw someone working in the fields. Thinking it was Marty, he took his gun out of his pocket and said, "Hold it right where you are."

Terry the farmhand got real scared, turned around, and

put his hands up. Zachary started towards Terry, who he thought was Marty because he was so far away. As Zachary got closer, he realized that it was Terry. He put his gun back in his pocket, walked over to Terry, and said, nervously, "Sorry, I thought you were Marty. I have found out who killed the Wilson family."

"Who was it?"

"Joe killed the parents and Suzanna. Marty killed Joe. Now Marty's on the loose."

Terry was very scared, afraid that he might be the next one. "But why did they kill each other?" he asked.

"Because of the inheritance. Joe killed his parents when he was eighteen. Now, seventeen years later, he killed Suzanna."

"This whole thing is crazy! I'm sick of this place." He threw his pitch fork across the field. "Let's get out of here. I know a little coffee shop on Box Avenue."

They both walked to Zachary's Blue Hornet. Zachary started the engine and drove off to the restaurant. As they got out of the car and walked into the restaurant, a man who was in the front seat of his car spotted them and put his foot on the gas pedal as fast as he could and drove off.

This man was Marty.

Chapter XVII: Marty

Half scared, Marty drove off into the heart of the town, and stopped at a very small, unnoticeable gas station. He drove his car to the back so no one could see it. He got out and walked into the men's room with a serviceman's jumpsuit in his hand. He took off his clothing and put the jumpsuit on. He brushed his hair and put some grease on his hands from a little bottle in his pocket. He looked like an attendant at a gas station.

Chapter XVIII: The Chase

After Zachary and Terry had finished their coffee, they drove off into the heart of town. Zachary looked down at the gas gauge, snapped his fingers and said, "I need some gas."

They came to a small gas station and pulled over. They sat in the car, but nobody came. He beeped his horn, but still nobody came.

"Damn it!" He beeped his horn again for a long time. And then a gas station attendant came out of the bathroom.

Zachary and Terry realized immediately that it was Marty. They both ran out of the car and tried to catch him, but Marty, seeing it was Terry and Zachary, ran to the back of the gas station. They heard a car start up, and then they ran back to their car and started their motor up. Just then Marty's car pulled out. Zachary pulled right in front of it and Marty crashed right into the side of Zachary's car.

Marty jumped out of his car and started running as fast as he could to the back of the gas station. Zachary chased him. Marty hid behind a tree and then made a run for the large open corn field behind the station. Zachary followed him close behind.

Just before Zachary was going to jump him, Marty jumped into a row of corn so Zachary couldn't see him. He saw some stalks of corn moving. At first he thought it was the wind, but then he saw a pair of feet. He walked slowly towards the rustling corn and made a jump for Marty and caught him by his legs. Marty put up a struggle, but Zachary soon overpowered him. Zachary put handcuffs on him and took him to his car.

"Why did you do it?"

"He killed my sister and my parents!" Marty screamed. "I'm not sorry I did it!"

Chapter XIX: The Confession

"I suspected Joe all along," Marty said in the police station. The bright lights were shining on his face. "Joe was a crazy kid. He used to put frogs in everyone's bed and snakes in the bathroom. He was very short-tempered. He told me our parents were always punishing him. They never let him go anywhere. He would go anyway. Then they would beat him with a belt. I suspected it."

"One night after Suzanna had been found dead, I saw Joe come home with a small book that had Suzanna's name on it. I knew right away that it was Suzanna's diary.

"I was curious to read it. I snuck into Joe's room while he was sleeping. He had left the diary on his dresser. I took it and went out into the barn. Finally I got to the last page and read what Suzanna said about a mask falling out of Joe's pocket. I ripped out the last two pages because I knew Joe would find out it was missing and would kill me next. I returned the diary to Suzanna's cottage, knowing that Zachary Smith would find it. I ripped out those pages and mailed them to Joshua so that if Joe killed me somebody else would know that Joe had killed Suzanna and our parents.

"He killed her with an old horseshoe he got from a pile of horseshoes we kept in the barn for the scrap metal man.

"I killed Joe because he was trying to frame me. He called you up, Zachary, saying that he knew who the murderer was. He still thought he had Suzanna's diary. He was going to forge her handwriting and show you a page that said I was going to kill Suzanna. I overheard him talking to himself about this plan to frame me. I felt like killing him.

"I stabbed him in the bedroom. He was looking at a poster of one of his favorite rock groups. His back was turned to the door. I crept in slowly with a kitchen knife and I stabbed him in the back. I heard Zachary Smith come in, so I left. I didn't know Joe was still alive.

"I'm glad I did it. I couldn't stand him. He was mean and

thoughtless to everyone, except himself."

Marty had a very serious face. His hair looked like a wet mop. In a very tired voice he said, "Please leave me alone now. I want to rest. I need to rest."

Chapter XX: Epilogue

Marty was put in jail for two years and then became an undercover detective.

Terry got married and had two kids. He inherited the farm and all the money.

Joshua Zoolosky became more successful than ever and stopped drinking.

Zachary became more famous, got a higher salary, became very rich, and went off to Hollywood, California, with his mother after cracking this case.

Zachary's mother died fourteen years later.

Several years after the case was solved, *the dog* was hit and run over by a car and was killed.

A lot of lives were wasted in this story.

Written by Wendy Pardew

With the help of:

Richard De Costa
Paul Wilson
Michael Kridler
Paul First
Chris Fisher
Landa Thompson
Antonio Dedivanovic

Confession

I did it. Now I am ashamed. I was in debt. He would not lend me the money I pleaded with him but he would not listen. My son was sick. He needed a liver transplant. I had finally convinced him to sign the papers which said I could have two thousand dollars for the operation. My own husband! Then he changed his mind. I was afraid he would tear it. He was standing on the balcony and I ran. He looked at my face then turned. In a sudden burst I grabbed for the paper and gave a hard shove. Over the balcony railing he went. I was shocked and sort of glad at the same time. I took the paper and ran out of the room. I don't remember how I felt inside. I know I was scared but my other emotions I just could not remember. I was his wife and I had killed.

—Susan Ward

The Killing of Jane Batista!

Jane Batista is missing. She was on her way to the store to get some blackeyed peas. Her mother found her gone when she went to the store to find out how come she (Jane) was gone. Her friend, Melissa, looked in the candy store. She could not find her! What could she do? She spent the whole day looking. So she went to the park. She looked in the playground, she looked in the sandbox.

Then: She saw a body in the pond, it was JANE! Oh, no! Not Jane! She was sobbing. She clung to the wet body, gooey with blood. She put her over her back and walked to the nearest store. The funeral was March 13, 1974.

The police suspected James E. Illingdon. The police found tracks in the mud. They followed the tracks, which ended in a hollow in the earth. Blood was smeared in these words: CAN YOU FIND OUT WHO DID IT? I DID! HA, HA! Then the tracks went on to the pond where Melissa said she found the body. It was all wet on the rocks from the splash of the body.

"I did it." An old man crawled from under the bush.

"Why?"

"Jane was a young and happy child. I am not happy! I despise happy people! So I killed her and I'm after you!" He pointed to Melissa. She hid behind a tree. All of a sudden he took out a gun and shot her.

A gasp rised among the police. They conned him into giving up the gun. They arrested him. They put him in the electric chair. He was gone. And so was Jane. And so was Melissa. So you see, nothing was solved.

But they don't know that it was another body with a plastic mask of Jane's face on it. And they don't know that Jane is still tied to a tree in the park a long long way from there, still screaming, screaming, screaming, screaming. . . .

—Melissa de Soto

Whodunit

There was something missing. Maybe something. But there was surely a missing subject on the estate of the Gremlodes. There were traces of blood on the sofa . . . and no fingerprints anywhere. There were sounds of murmuring and the clicking of the reporter's cameras. A frightened figure stood in the middle of the room. She was wearing a black dress and a white laced apron. Her hands were trembling. And her eyes were like round balls of fire.

"Ms. Farley, where were you at the time of the incident?" the inspector asked in a suspecting way.

The maid stuttered. "W-why, I was out buying lettuce and p-potatoes." Her hands were fidgeting with her apron, flapping it up and down.

The inspector sighed. "Wasn't there anyone else here?"

The maid replied, "Well, b-before I left, Mr. Gremlodes' wife was here. The cook was, too."

The tall inspector was becoming impatient. "I see." He took notes down. "Did Mr. Gremlodes have any enemies?" The maid picked her shoulders up and dropped them. They both stirred as they heard a shout.

"Oh, no!! My diamond tiara! It's gone! It's gone!"

There were cops running up the stairs. They then heard a scream. It was loud. It was very loud. It came from Mrs. Gremlodes! When they came to her room, they found Mrs. Gremlodes' face hidden in her hands. And on the floor was the body of Fenston Gremlodes.

The people came to the frightened Mrs. Gremlodes. They gasped at the sight of the body. Some ladies fainted: some men had to hold their stomachs.

The body had bloody scratches over itself. Scratches that didn't look human. Scratches that spelled terror. Scratches that looked as if a cat's claws came upon it.

In the police station, everyone was there: the inspector, Mrs. Gremlodes, Ms. Farley, the cook, and the neighbors. It was a distinguishing scene: Mrs. Gremlodes crying, Ms. Farley shuddering, the cook calm and looking at his nails, and the neighbors whispering and nudging each other.

The inspector McDowall was speaking to the chief. "But why would a cat and how could a cat steal a diamond tiara?! You tell me that!" exclaimed the chief.

McDowall tried to explain. "I didn't say that. Maybe the killer had a cat."

"Yeah, uh-huh, sure. What would he do with a cat if he knew he could murder the poor guy himself, eh?"

McDowall gave up. He turned to the group. "Did you ever keep a cat in the house?"

Everyone looked at each other. "No," answered Mrs. Gremlodes.

Ms. Farley glared at Mrs. Gremlodes. She caught it. "But the c-cook has one, don't you, Hans?" She sniffed.

Hans looked at her. "I used to. Me little darlin's daid now."

"Alright. You folks can go back home now," McDowall told them.

Soon it was night, and McDowall decided to walk home instead of taking the bus. While he was strolling, he passed the lake. He saw something shining. He bent over to reach it, but he found it was too far out floating in the lake. He then pulled a branch from a tree, and tried to bring this shiny object to him. He was curious to know what it was . . . and then . . . he was even more curious in *why* it was. Because it was a . . . diamond tiara! He turned around, he heard someone yell.

"Hey, Mister!" A fat man came to join him. He was round as a dumpling. "Name's Smith. I work at a gas station near here."

"Well, what do you want?" McDowall asked.

"Aren't you inspector McDowall who's working on that Gremlodes case?"

McDowall became interested. "Yes . . ." Smith settled down in the grass.

"Well, Mr. Gremlodes used to come down to my station often. He used to tell me about the troubles he had with his wife."

"Indeed?"

"Yeah." He sounded like a New Yorker. (This was England.) "And just the other day I saw him throw that tiara in the lake, but he didn't know it."

McDowall looked at him. "How do I know you're telling the truth?" But McDowall knew. Smith had the most honest eyes McDowall had ever seen.

"If you come to my gas station, I'll show you the broken door I had to replace for Mr. Gremlodes."

McDowall replied, "I'll come. And why are you telling me this?"

Smith smiled. "My father was once an inspector like you.

He always told me to help the law, and the law'll help you. Maybe you knew him. His name was Mike Smith."

McDowall thought for awhile. "Smith . . . Smith . . . I don't think so . . . wait! Yes! Mike Smith! Wasn't he the fellow who broke the kidnaping case in 1956?"

"That's my dad," the man replied proudly.

"Yes. When I was young I'd see his name in the paper a lot. I never really knew him."

When they reached the gas station, Smith told him all he knew about Mr. Gremlodes. Then he showed McDowall the broken car door.

McDowall nodded. "I'd like you to come with me tomorrow."

In the morning Smith and McDowall went to the Gremlodes estate. They were greeted by Ms. Farley.

"The missus is out in the garden with a strange man. She says she doesn't want to be disturbed."

McDowall winked at Smith. "She'll see us," he told her. "But don't TELL her we're here. It's very important."

Smith and McDowall went to the garden. They hid behind the bushes next to where Mrs. Gremlodes and the man sat. While the two had their conversation, McDowall taped it.

"You were brilliant, Nancy. That McDowall guy didn't suspect a thing!"

"Well, Hans, I needed your help to wipe Fenston out," said Mrs. Gremlodes laughing. "Soon, we'll be off to Mexico and no one will know how old Fenston was murdered."

"Except us, of course," Hans kissed her on the cheek.

"Of course," Nancy laughed. "You still do have that cat, don't you?"

"Me darlin's very much alive," he chuckled.

Nancy sighed. "I do wish I knew where my tiara is!" Hans placed his hand in hers.

"With all the money we have from Fenston? I'll buy you another—10 times better!"

Then McDowall came out of the bushes. "You won't have

to. I have it right here."

Nancy gasped. Hans looked furious. Smith handcuffed them. McDowall played the tape. When it was through, McDowall told them, "You're under arrest for the murder of Fenston Gremlodes."

—Cece Lee

Adventure Stories

Joey and myself are now sitting in a camouflaged tent in the Sinai desert. We're looking for our rendezvous man. "Joey, you get Headquarters on the horn while I shoot a flare." Klik Choofl. The red flare gleamed in the night air. Joey got HQ on the radio. They told him we'd see him soon. I spotted a silver object lying in the sand. I grabbed the spotlight and panned around. I got its position and dashed for it, then when I got to it, I saw our rendezvous man was here. It was one hell of a tape recorder! It was a large reel-to-reel gizmo. As I heaved it back to the tent, Joey clicked the radio back on. "All right, HQ, he's here," he said. I threw the PLAY switch. "Good morning, Phil, Joey," I looked at my watch, it was three o'clock. "As you know we're (the CIA) trying to find out about the assassinations that are being done all over this wasteland called the Middle East. We think the killings are somehow connected. They all have used the same method. Long range .223 rifle shot. Obviously fired from a rooftop. Your mission is to foil and uncover the killer or killers. This tape and the machine will blow up in 13 seconds. 12 - 11 - 10 - 9 - 8 - 7 I grabbed it and flung it outside the tent. 6 - 5 - 4 Bazoom! It was disintegrated. There were pieces all over the place! "Bad timer" I said.

Beirut, Lebanon. Two days later. The street fighting between sects is still raging. The day before, the Lebanese prime minister had resigned. This meant more sectarian fighting. He wanted to form a government made of both groups. This made him a prime target. This was so because this assassinating "ring" had been killing leaders that were important to their countries. The next day the prime minister was to leave the country for St. Moritz, Switzerland, to go skiing. He was to go on a public airliner. Incognito. We were going to get onto this plane and pose as a ski patrol at Saint Moritz. Then there was trouble. The plane got hijacked. This guy must have done it many times before. He had a sonic transmitter which was for a large supply of TNT which he had hid somewhere. All he had to do to blow us up is press a button. Joey had slipped his rifle out of its case and loaded it. He rested the barrel on the headrest in front of us. The skyjacker was checking with the crew and as soon as he whirled around, Joey cut him down. The prime minister, who was a good athelete himself, dove for the transmitter as it plummetted, button-first. The passengers thanked Joey for his quick thinking and markmanship.

St. Moritz. We went up the ski lift at about 1:30. Joey was looking around the trees, for snipers. I spotted the prime minister taking lessons. We played dummy for awhile watching him learn to stop. The prime minister decided to go down the beginner slope. Then a skiier who had been going up the lift, lifted a .223, bam! a bullet ripped a hole in the prime minister's chest. Joey tore after him. I skied down to the ski patrol station and grabbed a rifle and jumped into a helicopter. "Hey!" said a patroller, running after me. I hit him in the head with a ski. Meanwhile Joey was pursuing the assassin. I started the chopper and took off. I spotted the killer and hovered over him. I had him in my sights, but he stopped and surrendered.

We got to the place where this guy's hideout was. He said there were more people and ammo there. We turned him over to the authorities. We were skiing down a back trail when a shotgun rang out. Pellets tore into my leg. Joey scooped me up and took off. I found myself in a hospital. I recovered in a few days. We flew back to the east and rested up. One night we went to the place the assassin had told us of. Joey, who had a rifle, clicked a grenade launcher onto his muzzle and launched a gas grenade through a window. I was on the roof of this small building. My plan was to create a diversion, the grenade and get the drop on em. The gas brought them outside with a lot hardware. Joey, seeing this, jumped on a barrel, climbed on a pipe and got on a roof. The terrorists hid behind everything. But me and Joey were in a crossfire so they surrenderred.

So much for that mission

—Sulli

Adventure

One day when I was taking my dog on a walk I met a very old lady sitting on a bench. I sat on the same bench the old lady was sitting on. I was patting my dog when I heard something falling down. I looked up and saw that the old lady had dropped her umbrella and couldn't bend over to get it. I left my dog and picked up the old lady's umbrella.

She thanked me. In a little while the old lady and I became very acquainted.

We began to talk about each other. She told me she was 86 years old. That she had no one in the world. And that her name was Ms. Grimwell. I felt very sad when I heard Ms.

Grimwell say that she had no one in the world. I told Ms. Grimwell about myself.

After I finished telling her about my life she told me what had happened to her when she was my age. She said, "When I was your age I was very beautiful. As you know I was born in England. My family was very wealthy.

"One day I was walking by the streets of London, England, and two men came and grabbed me by the arm and closed my mouth with his hand. They did this so fast I didn't have time to scream. The two men grabbed me and pushed me into a black autmobile. They stopped and took me out and pushed me toward a small dusty house. The man took his hand off my face and said, 'Now you can talk because nobody will hear you. There is not one bloody soul around here.'

"When I heard this I almost fainted. 'You know what we're going to do to you, we are going to take you to another country,' said one of the men. I answered, 'W . . . hy?' 'Because your father is very rich and we don't want him to be rich. He is going to have to pay a lot of money for you because I've spent a lot of money for kidnaping you,' another man answered. 'Now we have to lock you up till tomorrow when we will be leaving for the United States,' he continued.

"They grabbed me by the arm and threw me in a room. They locked the room with a key and walked away. In the room there was a gas lamp, a bed and a small window with bars over it. I got in the bed and started to cry.

"The next thing I knew I heard the two men coming in the door. I guess I must have fallen asleep. I got in the car again. They told me if I said anything they would kill me. We left England and landed in the U.S.A. There the two men left me all alone. A lot of people helped me as the years passed until I got old and began to work so I could live. I never knew what had happened to my family." Tears were coming out of the old lady's eyes. She left the bench. I never saw her again.

—Ingrid Arias

221

My Friend, King Neptune

One day, I went swimming with my family at a beach. Since I had learned how to swim, I thought I'd show off. So I started swimming; but all of a sudden a big wave came along and the current swept me far out. Then came another big wave and it put me under water. Down, down, down I went. Somehow I was breathing.

After ten or fifteen minutes, I hit some sand. Little fish were wiggling all around me. I decided to explore. Just as I was getting up, a friendly dolphin came over to me. We started to swim around; I saw a beautiful shell in the sand. By mistake the dolphin pushed me down onto the sand and wouldn't you know, I fell into a hole; and further down I went.

Everything was black. I couldn't see a thing. After a few minutes of falling I fell into a soft cuddly thing that felt like a chair. Suddenly there was light, just as I fell on the chair. I looked around and there stood an old man with a long white beard, a scepter in his hand, and two sting rays, four sharks and an octopus surrounding him.

"Who are you?" I said. He said, "I am King Neptune." He took me by the hand and showed me his kingdom. He said that I was his first visitor. He said that he was very lonely, and that he'd like me to visit him sometime. Just then I thought of my mother and father. They did not know where I was. I told the king this, and with a stamp of his foot I was standing on the beach.

—Donna Beasley

The Time Machine

Once there was a guy his name was Alfred. He had a wife, Beth. They had one boy, John, and one girl, Susan, 9 and 10.

The father was a scientist. He made very great inventions. He was well known through the country. Not for chemicals, but he worked with electronics. One day he was inventing in his laboratory and he realized that it was possible to make a time machine. He spent about fifty straight hours working on the plans to make it. He finished the plans and began working on the time machine. A day later it was finished. It was a big square box about 5 by 5. Outside it was a little gizmo with buttons. The door looked like a vault door. It looked like a rectangle safe, about the size to fit two grown ups.

He had kept it a secret for a year or two. One day he said, Kids I have a surprise for you. I invented a time machine. I'll show you it. But you must promise not to tell anyone or I'll be mobbed. And never go in it and press the stuff on the outside.

That night the kids went downstairs. And they OPENED THE DOOR. They pressed a couple of buttons on the outside and hopped in. It started making funny noises after they were inside. Then they started feeling a dizzy feeling. And then all of a sudden all the noises stopped and it didn't feel like they were moving anymore. They climbed out of the box and found themselves in the American Revolution. They were right in the middle of the meeting when they decided for Paul Revere to go to the old church. Then they were found and thought as spies. They were brought to the British headquarters, and they put them in jail and they squeezed through the bars since they were very small. And then they were free and they ran a back to their time machine. And pressed another couple of buttons.

Then they went through that same dizzy feeling again and heard those noises and then it stopped. They opened the door and found themselves facing a castle. They saw the drawbridge lower. They saw about fifty knights on horseback and then about five hundred on foot following them and then up on the peak of the castle they could see the king. They climbed up a high tree and could see another approaching army. Then all of a sudden they clashed together. It was a horrible sight. Men falling all over the place. And then all of a sudden one side had won. All these hoorays and cheers had come from the side that won. The children ducked back into the bushes as what was left of the army went back into the castle.

The children ran back to the time machine with four knights chasing after them on horsback. They quickly made it into the time machine, and pressed a few buttons and all of a sudden they felt that dizzy weird feeling and those loud noises. And when it stopped they opened the door.

They saw a dinosaur. It was a Terrenidon with horns. It looked like a bull. They had seen pictures of it in history class at school except that it was about fifty times bigger than a bull. Then all of sudden we saw all these tiny dinosaurs. All of a sudden this big chase took place and all the dinosaurs started chasing us. And then we found a small cave where we could just barely squeeze in and nothing else could squeeze in. The dinosaurs were too fat. But they were waiting outside so we had no way of getting back to the time machine. We looked behind us and saw that we weren't in a cave, but in a tunnel obviously made by a man because it looked like it was kind of dug out by shells and things. On the other side we saw tyrannosaurus rex waiting for us. We waited another night. And we got very hungry. Then on another side of the wall we saw a crack and we barely squeezed through and we ran to the time machine and pressed another couple of buttons and all of a sudden we felt that dizzy weird feeling again and then it stopped. We opened the door. And we were home! It was in the middle of the night. We went back to sleep and forgot about it and kept it a secret and no one ever knew about it. We had a good time for the rest of our lives.

By Adam Yauch & Matthew Allison

Romance Stories

I met you in the coffee shop. I asked you for a date. You said no, then you broke my heart. I didn't really care because I was going to ask you again. I knew you wouldn't turn me down, that's why I asked you again. I love you so deeply with all my heart. The sweetness in your face makes me feel so fine. But when you turn me down again I feel like I lose my heart and it was not beating. I thought for a while and I said to myself he really loves me or else you must hate me. If you do hate me I will still love you so.

—Sherrae Givens

Let Me Die

Linda Rogers was combing her hair. "Tomorrow's the last day. I commit suicide," thought Linda. "But why Linda?" she asked herself as she put down her comb and strode into the bathroom. "I know why I wanna kill myself . . . because of Jeff!" She banged her fist down on the marble. "Ouch!" she screamed. "Why did he leave me? . . . Oh Jeff don't you see I love you . . . I need you too . . . or I used to!"

She went into the kitchen and fixed herself a piece of toast. She began to butter her toast as she thought of Jeff. She scraped off some of the butter and said through a mouthful of toast, "Why wait till tomorrow? Okay! I will kill myself today. . . ." She went to get her butcher knife and thought aloud, "I want this to be public. . . . I want Jeff to hear about this and think, "Why didn't I stay with Linda? . . . Or this wouldn't have happened!" She laughed gleefully. She put down her toast and put on her best clothes. She wanted to die beautiful. She went to the roof (29 floors high) and stood there for twenty minutes. A woman across the street called the firemen. Linda heard the sirens and jumped. Right into the fireman's arms. "Let me die," she shouted over 16 times and fainted. They put her in hospital. She fell in love with the fireman and is happily married.

—Melissa DeSotto and
Ally Vega

The Teacher That Bought the Vase on Lexington Avenue

Once there was a teacher whose name was Ms. Slax. She taught in a school called "The Henry Kissinger School." Everyone there, including the teachers (especially the men), thought she was the prettiest woman in the school. It was true, too! She had wavy, red hair that she washed twice a week, a perfect figure, and really beautiful clothes. Anyway, all the men in the school (including the principal, Mr. Simon Peabody) kept sending her bouquets of flowers. They were crazy over her! But poor Ms. Slax! She was running out of vases to put all the flowers in! First she used up all her vases, then her glass glasses, and finally, paper cups! "Oh dear!" she sighed, "I've used all my vases, glasses and cups! And just got another bouquet! Oh dear!" Then she had an idea. "I know what I'll do!" she cried, "I'll go down to Lexington Avenue and get a new vase!" And that's exactly what she did.

As she was strolling down Lexington Avenue, she met Mr.

226

Charlston, a teacher in her school. "Why hello, Mary!" he said. Mary Slax was her name. "Please Ben, don't call me Mary," she said. "Very well, Ms. Slax, if you say so!" he said. Ms. Slax smiled. "Where're you going?" Mr. Charlston asked. "I can't tell you," she replied, and went on her way. Mr. Charlston looked after her, scratched his head, and sighed. Then he turned and went his way.

Ms. Slax stopped in front of an antique shop. There were no vases in the window. "Oh dear," sighed Ms. Slax, and walked on.

Finally she came to a store called "Wilson's Vase and Pot Store." "Oh good!" exclaimed Ms. Slax. "I think I found what I've been looking for!" Then she opened the door and went in. The shop was very big. There were billions of shelves, with billions of pots of all kinds sitting on them. And, of course, vases of all kinds, shapes, and sizes. "Oh, this is just what I've been looking for! I'm so glad I've come!" She looked around. There were so many vases to choose from! Then a man came out from behind a counter somewhere and came up to her. He thought she was pretty, too. He had a long, black moustache that he twisted thoughtfully and slick, black hair. It was clear to see that he was Italian. "Ah, Miss, may I help you?" he asked with an Italian accent. Ms. Slax turned around. "Oh, why y-yes, you can!" she stammered. She had been startled. "What are you looking for, Miss?" inquired the clerk. He was liking Ms. Slax more and more, and feeling glad that he was a bachelor. "Perhaps," he thought, "she will come out with me tonight!" Ms. Slax replied, "Oh, I'm just looking for a nice vase to put some flowers in." She did not say just where she had gotten them from. "Ah yes, a vase. Does madame want any particular pattern?"

"No, not really."

"Hm-m-m-m." He twisted his moustache. "Let me see. Ah! I know! Come over here, madame, over here." Oh how he liked Ms. Slax! And, Ms. Slax was beginning to, well, admire him too! "Sir," she asked, "How should I address you?" He turned to face her. "Just call me Antonio, Anthony for short. What should I call you?" Ms. Slax was so surprised that at first she didn't answer. Then she said, "Just call me Mary." The very name she had told Mr. Charlston *not* to address her by! "Very well, then, Miss, ah, Mary, I have just what you want, I think." By now he was head-over-heels in love with her. And she with him too! Well, Antonio showed her a vase, a really beautiful one, with porcelain with tiny roses and daisies painted on it. "Ohhh!" exclaimed Ms. Slax when she saw it. "I want it! I want it!!" she exclaimed. "Oh, I do!" And so she did. And . . . as Antonio was wrapping it up, she asked, a little shyly, "Would you like to come to dinner with me tonight?" Antonio looked up and smiled a white-toothed smile. "If madame will have me," said he.

It was the beginning of a wonderful friendship.

—Yvonne S. Kingon

Marriage Proposal

Prince John:	Will you marry me, Princess Joanne?
Princess Joanne:	How did you know my name?
Prince John:	Your mother and my mother are good friends.
Princess Joanne:	I will marry you, Prince John. When are we getting married, darling?
Prince John:	Late tonight—around 12 o'clock.
Queen Sonia:	I am so glad you got married.
Queen Joanne:	I am glad you found a man.
Prince John:	Let's go home, darling.
Princess Joanne:	Sure thing, darling.
King Mark:	Joanne, what is your husband's name?
Princess Joanne:	His name is John.
King Mark:	Is Princess Joanne pretty?

Prince John:	Yes. Now we are going to my palace where I have a maid.
Princess Joanne:	I'd love to live there. Let's go to bed. I am awfully tired, and we have to get up early.
Prince John:	I agree.

(Prince John is now King Johnny; Princess Joanne is Queen Joany.)

King Johnny:	Darling, it is time to get up.
Queen Joany:	Thank you for waking me up.
King Johnny:	Do you want to have a baby?
Queen Joany:	I'd love it.
Queen Joany:	I had a girl, darling.
King Johnny:	I am glad we have a new princess in the family. Let's name her Jody.
Queen Joany:	I love that name.
King Johnny:	I am really glad you love it, because I love that name also.
King Johnny:	Do you want to have another kid?
Queen Joany:	Yeah, I'm trying for a boy.
King Johnny:	You'll have a boy, I know it.
Queen Joany:	I am sorry our kids don't have grandparents.
King Johnny:	I am sorry their grandparents died.
Queen Joany:	I had a boy.
King Johnny:	I told you you would have a boy.
Queen Joany:	Let's name the baby Paul.
King Johnny:	I love that name. Just imagine—Prince Paul. How wonderful it sounds. Do you want me to get you a drink?
Queen Joany:	Yes, I am very tired from the baby.
King Johnny:	I know. Now, why don't you rest, sweetheart?
Queen Joany:	Get me the baby's bottles.

King Johnny:	Both of them?
Queen Joany:	Yes, both of them.
King Johnny:	Maid! Get me the two baby bottles.
Maid:	Here they are, sir.
King Johnny:	Thank you, maid.
Maid:	You're welcome, sir.

(Maid's name is Joyce.)

King Johnny:	Darling, Jody is crying again.
Queen Joany:	I'll take care of her, darling.
King Johnny:	Do you want some food for her?
Queen Joany:	I would love it, darling.
King Johnny:	Today is Jody's birthday.
Queen Joany:	Yes, I know. She is two years old.
Princess Jody:	Mommy, please get me down a cup and a drink.
Queen Joany:	Sure, Princess Jody. Today you are two years old.
Princess Jody:	How old is Paul?
Queen Joany:	One year old in May, 1974.
Queen Joany:	Maid, bring the cake, please. Thank you, maid.
Maid:	You're welcome.
All:	Happy birthday to you, Happy birthday to you, Happy birthday, dear Jody, Happy birthday to you.
Queen Joany:	Jody, blow out all the candles.
Princess Jody:	Thank you, Mommy and Dada.
Queen Joany:	You're welcome.
King Johnny:	You're welcome.
Queen Joany:	I'll cut the cake for you.
King Johnny:	(Whisper) Give Joyce a small piece. She is too fat.
Queen Joany:	I agree about that. Can I give Jody a big piece?
King Johnny:	Give her a medium piece, honey.

Queen Joany:	I will do what you say, darling.
Maid:	I don't want a piece of cake.
Queen Joany:	I love birthday parties.
King Johnny:	I love birthday parties, especially for my children.
Queen Joany:	I like them for my kids, also.
Princess Jody:	Thank you for the party, Mom. Also you, Dad.
Queen Joany:	You're welcome, I am very proud of you.
King Johnny:	You're welcome, Jody. I am proud, too.
Princess Jody:	Why are you proud of me, Mom? You, too, Dad?
Parents:	Because you entertained your friends so well. Let's give Paul a chance to be one year old.
Queen Joany:	Let's bring out the cake and sing happy birthday to Paul.
All:	Happy birthday to you, Happy birthday to you, Happy birthday, dear Paul, Happy birthday to you.
Queen Joany:	Blow out the candles.
Prince Paul:	Okay, Mommy.
Queen Joany:	I am a proud mother.

—Sabrina Kurtin

Love in London

The streets of London seemed strange, eerie, and foggy as Emily walked along the pavement of Ponce Street. It seemed unreal and make-believe that she could be in London. She had spent her whole life in New York and she had to move because of her father's china business. It had been two weeks since she had been in New York. How could she make new friends? "Will they accept me in school? I wonder if I'll meet a boyfriend?" In school, in New York, she was known as being good with the boys. They liked her and she had a lot of boyfriends.

She had seen some girls walking up Ponce Street and she tried to join them but she didn't know how to approach them. As they entered the school gates she felt more lost in herself, confused, with no one to talk to and no one to say her problems to.

She was in her class now and wondering if her father would be waiting for her at the china shop so they could walk home together. The bell interrupted her thoughts. As she lifted her books, she felt as if someone was watching her. Clumsily, she dropped her books. A boy anxiously picked them up. "New around here?" Before her stood a boy, intelligent looking, clean cut and very polite. His hair was combed to the side, his deep blue eyes seemed radiant and his sharp clothes stood out more than ever. He was all dressed up with a tie and a velvet jacket. "He is the kind of boy who is popular and would introduce me to new friends," she thought.

"Oh! Thank you. I didn't have my mind on what I was doing."

"You're welcome. It was nothing. I'll always lend a hand if it is needed."

As she walked out the class to go into another, she saw girls her age who she thought weren't the friends she should meet. They seemed immature as they laughed and ran through the halls. She went, going about her business and keeping to herself, to the other class. Then finally a girl who looked as lost as she did approached her and asked anxiously, "Where's the reading room?" Emily thought, "Here's my chance to make a friend." She replied, "I don't really know. I'm new here too. My name is Emily. What's yours?"

"Marcy! Marcy Cummings. I'm a freshman here at Beverly

Hall. Do you live close around here?" asked Marcy.

"Yes. Right off Ponce Street."

"Oh great! I live on Falls Lane, just around the corner from your house." Marcy said, "Hey, have you seen the new sophomore?"

"Gee, I don't know. How does he look?"

"Well, he's tall, nice dressed, has blue eyes and is well mannered. And he has brown hair to the side."

"Gee, he sounds familiar. I think he's the boy who picked up my books."

Marcy replied, "Walter picked up *your* books? He doesn't usually make a pass to a girl that fast."

"Is he shy?"

"No, but he's supposed to be someone special."

Just then as Emily turned around, Walter walked slowly across the hall, winking his eye.

"Hi Marcy! Aren't you going to introduce us?"

"Walter, this is Emily. Emily, this is Walter."

"What are you girls up to?"

"We were just on our way home."

"Those books look heavy. Mind if I carry them, Emily?"

"Sure. Thanks!"

As they passed the gates of the school, Emily just remembered she had to stop by her father's shop.

Marcy said to herself, "This is a good chance to be alone with Walter." She said to Emily, "Where are you going now? Are you going straight home?"

"I'm going to my father's shop. Would you like to come?"

Marcy said, "I've got to hurry home and finish my math assignment."

Walter, seeming confused, said, "Whose books do I have?"

"Oh, those are mine. They are pretty heavy," Emily said. "Well, I guess I'll be going."

"I'll walk with you because I have to pass there anyway."

"What about Marcy," Emily, being thoughtful, asked.

Walking towards the china shop, they stopped and Walter

asked, "What are you doing Saturday night. You know there's that big dance."

Emily thought, "I don't know if I should, Marcy seems attached to him and if I do go with him, Marcy will resent me. But he does seem like a nice boy. I think I will go with him."

"Sure, Walter, I'd love to." She thought, "Look! My first day in school and I've already found a boy I like. Things aren't going that bad at all." She didn't even know why he took a liking to her so fast. Gee, I must really like him, she thought. I get butterflies in my stomach when I see him. I feel embarrassed to show my true feeling toward him because maybe I'm not good enough for him, being that he dresses so well and has such good manners. I even wonder if his intentions are good.

Saturday night finally came. She was all dressed up in her pink gown and was still fixing her hair.

The door bell rang. "That must be Walter. I must hurry up."

Her father answered the door.

"Hello. You must be Walter. My daughter has talked about you often. Sit down. She will be ready in just a minute. Emily!" her father yelled up, "Walter's here!"

"What are your intentions with my daughter? She's a very quiet girl and was brought up simple. What are you going to be doing tonight?"

"Well, we're going dancing at the annual dance at Beverly Hall."

"I want you home before eleven."

Walter felt guilty of not doing nothing. After the lecture Walter had a hunch that the father didn't like him, but that was not to think about now, for him and Emily liked each other a lot.

Suddenly Emily hurried down the stairs. Walter approached her, took the corsage and gently pinned it on her evening dress. Emily said, "Gee, it matches my dress perfectly." She had a lot of boyfriends in New York, but they had not treated her as well as Walter did. Walter treated her more mature.

"Goodnight, Mr. Edwards. We'll be home at eleven."

"Have a nice time."

*

Now at Beverly Hall, all the girls seemed to look beautiful. Their gowns were all very elegant, and stylish. Suddenly the lights seemed dimmer and the music seemed softer. They were starting to dance closer and closer as Emily realized she was now really in love. All the girls must envy Emily and you can bet Marcy had her eyes on them all evening.

All of a sudden them two were the center of attraction and the only two dancing on the floor. They were in a trance with their love and didn't care what Marcy and the other girls thought about them.

Dancing alone, getting farther from the crowd, they stopped and Walter said, "How much time flies when you are dancing with someone special." Walter suddenly reached for the bracelet on his arm and gently placed it on her wrist. The heavy sterling links were still warm from his wrist. He looked up at Emily and said, "Do you know what this means when a boy gives his name bracelet to his date?"

Emily replied, "Yes. I do. It means that we're going steady."

As he approached her, he slowly put his arm around her. He finally kissed Emily. She never thought a boy's lips could be so tender. She was Walter's girl and that's all that really mattered.

by Marcia Lanza, 13½ and Livia Scotto, 14

Teachers & Writers Publications

THE WHOLE WORD CATALOGUE 1 (72 pages) is a practical collection of assignments for stimulating student writing, designed for both elementary and secondary students. Activities designed as catalysts for classroom exercises include: personal writing, collective novels, diagram stories, fables, spoof and parodies, and language games. It also contains an annotated bibliography.

THE WHOLE WORD CATALOGUE 2 edited by Bill Zavatsky and Ron Padgett (350 pages). A completely new collection of writing and art ideas for the elementary, secondary, and college classroom. Deepens and widens the educational ground broken by our underground best seller, the first *Whole Word Catalogue*. Order two copies and get a free subscription for a friend.

IMAGINARY WORLDS (110 pages) originated from Richard Murphy's desire to find themes of sufficient breadth and interest to allow sustained, independent writing by students. Children invented their own Utopias of time and place, invented their own religions, new ways of fighting wars, different schools. They produced a great deal of extraordinary writing, much of it reprinted in the book.

A DAY DREAM I HAD AT NIGHT (120 pages) is a collection of oral literature from children who were not learning to read well or write competently or feel any real sense of satisfaction in school. The author, Roger Landrum, working in collaboration with two elementary school teachers, made class readers out of the children's own work.

FIVE TALES OF ADVENTURE (119 pages) is a new collection of short novels written by children at a Manhattan elementary school. The stories cover a wide range of styles and interests—a family mystery, an urban satire, a Himalayan adventure, a sci-fi spoof, and a tale of murder and retribution.

TEACHING AND WRITING POPULAR FICTION: HORROR, ADVENTURE, MYSTERY AND ROMANCE IN THE AMERICAN CLASSROOM by Karen Hubert (236 pages). A new step-by-step guide on using the different literary genres to help students to write, based on the author's intensive workshops conducted for Teachers & Writers in elementary and secondary schools. Ms. Hubert explores the psychological necessities of each genre and discusses the various ways of tailoring each one to individual students. Includes hundreds of "recipes" to be used as story starters, with an anthology of student work to show the exciting results possible.

JUST WRITING (104 pages) by Bill Bernhardt. A book of exercises designed to make the reader aware of all the necessary steps in the writing process. This book can be used as a do-it-yourself writing course. It is also an invaluable resource for writing teachers.

TO DEFEND A FORM (211 pages) by Ardis Kimzey. Tells the inside story of administering a poets-in-the-schools program. It is full of helpful procedures that will insure a smoothly running program. The book also contains many classroom-tested ideas to launch kids into poetry writing and an extensive bibliography of poetry anthologies and related material indispensable to anyone who teaches poetry.

BEING WITH CHILDREN, a book by Phillip Lopate, whose articles have appeared regularly in our magazine, is based on his work as project coordinator for Teachers & Writers Collaborative at P.S. 75 in Manhattan. Herb Kohl writes: "There is no other book that I know that combines the personal and the practical so well...." *Being With Children* is published by Doubleday at $7.95. It is available through Teachers & Writers Collaborative for $4.00. Paperback $1.95.

VERMONT DIARY (180 pages) by Marvin Hoffman. Describes the process of setting up a writing center within a rural elementary school. The book covers a two year period during which the author and several other teachers endeavor to build a unified curriculum based on the language arts.

THE POETRY CONNECTION by Nina Nyhart and Kinereth Gensler. This is a collection of adult and children's poetry with strategies to get students writing, an invaluable aid in the planning and execution of any poetry lesson.

TEACHERS & WRITERS Magazine, issued three times a year, draws together the experience and ideas of the writers and other artists who conduct T & W workshops in schools and community groups. A typical issue contains excerpts from the detailed work diaries and articles of the artists, along with the works of the students and outside contributions.

☐ The Whole Word Catalogue 2 @ $6.95
☐ The Whole Word Catalogue 1 @ $4.00
☐ Teaching & Writing Popular Fiction @ $4.00
☐ Being With Children @ $4.00
☐ Five Tales of Adventure @ $3.00 (10 copies or more @ $2.00)
☐ Imaginary Worlds @ $3.00
☐ A Day Dream I Had at Night @ $3.00
☐ Just Writing @ $4.00
☐ To Defend a Form @ $4.00
☐ Vermont Diary @ $4.00
☐ The Poetry Connection @ $4.00
☐ Subscription(s) to **T&W Magazine**, three issues $5.00, six issues $9.00, nine issues $12.00

NAME _____

ADDRESS_____

☐ Please make checks payable to Teachers & Writers Collaborative, and send to:
    Teachers & Writers   TOTAL
    84 Fifth Avenue   ENCLOSED
    New York City 10011 $_____